Wall Street
in Transition

THE CHARLES C. MOSKOWITZ LECTURES NUMBER XV

Henry G. Manne

DISTINGUISHED PROFESSOR OF LAW,
DIRECTOR OF THE CENTER FOR STUDIES IN
LAW AND ECONOMICS
UNIVERSITY OF MIAMI LAW SCHOOL

Ezra Solomon

DEAN WITTER PROFESSOR OF FINANCE
STANFORD UNIVERSITY

Wall Street in Transition

The Emerging System and Its Impact on the Economy

THE CHARLES C. MOSKOWITZ LECTURES
COLLEGE OF BUSINESS AND PUBLIC ADMINISTRATION
NEW YORK UNIVERSITY

NEW YORK   *New York University Press*   1974

FOREWORD

The Charles C. Moskowitz Lectures are arranged by the College of Business and Public Administration of New York University and aim at advancing public understanding of the issues that are of major concern to business and the nation. Established through the generosity of Mr. Charles C. Moskowitz, a distinguished alumnus of the College and a former Vice President-Treasurer and Director of Loew's, Inc., they have enabled the College to make a significant contribution to public understanding of important issues facing the American economy and its business enterprises.

The fifteenth in the series of Charles C. Moskowitz Lectures was planned to focus on the theme "Wall Street in Transition: The Emerging

System and Its Impact on the Economy," and
provided a forum for four distinguished authorities to discuss that subject, Henry G. Manne,
formerly Kenan Professor of Law at the University of Rochester and presently Distinguished
Professor of Law and Director of the Center for
Studies in Law and Economics at the University
of Miami Law School, presented a paper on
"Economic Aspects of Required Disclosure
Under Federal Securities Laws," while Ezra
Solomon, Dean Witter Professor of Finance at
Stanford University, spoke on the "Impact of
the Emerging System on Securities Trading and
the Economy." Both papers were vigorously dis-
cussed by Kalman J. Cohen, presently Dis-
tinguished Bank Research Professor at the
Graduate School of Business Administration,
Duke University, and formerly Distinguished
Professor of Economics and Finance and Direc-
tor of the Salomon Brothers Institute for the
Study of Financial Institutions at New York
University's Graduate School of Business Administration, and William J. Baumol, Professor
of Economics at New York University and
Princeton University.

Interest in these lectures was particularly
high, since everyone was aware of the series of
shocks which the financial heartland of America
has suffered in recent years. And it was clear
that the long-established business customs and

institutions of Wall Street were bound to be profoundly changed as a consequence of those shocks. Given that context and some audience expectation of surprising statements by the speakers, Professor Manne still managed to jolt, perhaps even shock, many with his quite sweeping attack on regulation of the securities markets. I am certain that readers of this volume will find his paper no less stimulating than his immediate lecture audience did. I am certain, too, that they will find the incisive and cogent comments of Professors Cohen and Baumol equally stimulative of thought. Professor Solomon, while somewhat less "shocking" to his listeners than Professor Manne, was no less stimulating in the substance of his lecture. He focused on three major structural changes underway in the securities industry, i.e., (1) the expanding institutionalization of the market for common stocks; (2) the passing of fixed minimum brokerage commission rates; and (3) the appearance of a central market for common stocks. His lecture was lucid, and I know that the readers of this volume will find the published paper equally so. Interestingly, Professor Baumol found himself essentially in agreement with Professor Solomon's observations, concentrating therefore on Professor Manne's paper. However, Professor Cohen, while not disagreeing substantially with Professor Solomon, offered several significant observations of his own on additional important structural changes already underway which will impact heavily on Wall Street and the securities industry. Finally, the readers of this volume will enjoy a bonus, for Professors John G. McDonald and Ezra Solomon have allowed the inclusion of their paper, "A Note on the Two-Tier Market, 1970-1974."

As always, Mrs. Patricia Matthias, my administrative assistant, was responsible for the many details connected with the lectures, and I express my appreciation to her. I express appreciation also to the members of the faculty committee that provides wise counsel on the selection of topics and speakers, Professors Jules Backman, Ernest Bloch, and Ernest Kurnow. And my thanks go as well to the staff of the New York University Press.

Abraham L. Gitlow
Dean
College of Business and
Public Administration

June 1974

THE CHARLES C. MOSKOWITZ LEC-
TURES were established through the generosity
of a distinguished alumnus of the College of
Business and Public Administration, Mr. Charles
C. Moskowitz of the Class of 1914, who retired
after many years as Vice President-Treasurer and
a Director of Loew's Inc.

In establishing these lectures, it was Mr.
Moskowitz's aim to contribute to the understanding of the function of business and its
underlying disciplines in society by providing a
public forum for the dissemination of enlight-
ened business theories and practices.

The College of Business and Public Administration and New York University are deeply
grateful to Mr. Moskowtiz for his continued interest in, and contribution to, the educational
and public service program of his alma mater.

This volume is the fifteenth in the Moskowitz series. The earlier ones were:

February, 1961   *Business Survival in the Sixties*
Thomas F. Patton, President and Chief Executive Officer
Republic Steel Corporation

November, 1961 *The Challenges Facing Management*
Don G. Mitchell, President
General Telephone and Electronics Corporation

November, 1962 *Competitive Private Enterprise Under Government Regulation*
Malcolm A. MacIntyre, President
Eastern Air Lines

November, 1963 *The Common Market: Friend or Competitor?*
Jesse W. Markham, Professor of Economics, Princeton University
Charles E. Fiero, Vice President, The Chase Manhattan Bank
Howard S. Piquet, Senior Specialist in International Economics, Legislative Reference Service, The Library of Congress

November, 1964 *The Forces Influencing the American Economy*
Jules Backman, Research Professor of Economics, New York University

Martin R. Gainsbrugh, Chief Economist and Vice President, National Industrial Conference Board

November, 1965 *The American Market of the Future*
Arno H. Johnson, Vice President and Senior Economist, J. Walter Thompson Company
Gilbert E. Jones, President, IBM World Trade Corporation
Darrell B. Lucas, Professor of Marketing and Chairman of the Department, New York University

November, 1966 *Government Wage-Price Guideposts in the American Economy*
George Meany, President, American Federation of Labor and Congress of Industrial Organizations
Roger M. Blough, Chairman of the Board and Chief Executive Officer, United States Steel Corporation
Neil H. Jacoby, Dean, Graduate School of Business Administration, University of California at Los Angeles

November, 1967 *The Defense Sector in the American Economy*

Jacob K. Javits, United States Senator, New York

Charles J. Hitch, President, University of California

Arthur F. Burns, Chairman, Federal Reserve Board

November, 1968 *The Urban Environment: How It Can Be Improved*

William E. Zisch, Vice-chairman of the Board, Aerojet-General Corporation

Paul H. Douglas, Chairman, National Commission on Urban Problems

Professor of Economics, New School for Social Research

Robert C. Weaver, President, Bernard M. Baruch College of the City University of New York

Former Secretary of Housing and Urban Development

November, 1969 *Inflation: The Problems It Creates and the Policies It Requires*

Arthur M. Okun, Senior Fellow, The Brookings Institution

Henry H. Fowler, General Partner, Goldman, Sachs & Co.

Milton Gilbert, Economic Adviser, Bank for International Settlements

March, 1971   *The Economics of Pollution*
Kenneth E. Boulding, Professor of Economics, University of Colorado
Elvis J. Stahr, President, National Audubon Society
Solomon Fabricant, Professor of Economics, New York University
Former Director, National Bureau of Economic Research
Martin R. Gainsbrugh, Adjunct Professor of Economics, New York University
Chief Economist, National Industrial Conference Board

April, 1971   *Young America in the NOW World*
Hubert H. Humphrey, Senator from Minnesota
Former Vice President of the United States

April, 1972   *Optimum Social Welfare and Productivity: A Comparative View*
Jan Tinbergen, Professor of Development Planning, Netherlands School of Economics
Abram Bergson, George F. Baker Professor of Economics, Harvard University

Fritz Machlup, Professor of Economics, New York University

Oskar Morgenstern, Professor of Economics, New York University

April, 1973

Fiscal Responsibility: Tax Increases of Spending Cuts?

Paul McCracken, Edmund Ezra Day University, Professor of Business Administration, University of Michigan

Murray L. Weidenbaum, Edward Mallinckrodt Distinguished University Professor, Washington University

Lawrence S. Ritter, Professor of Finance, New York University

Robert A. Kavesh, Professor of Finance, New York University

CONTENTS

ECONOMIC ASPECTS OF REQUIRED DISCLOSURE UNDER FEDERAL SECURITIES LAWS

Henry G. Manne

Distinguished Professor of Law,
Director of the Center for Studies in
Law and Economics
University of Miami Law School

The author would like to acknowledge his appreciation for helpful suggestions made by Professor George Benston, Michael Jensen, and James Mofsky, though of course they are not responsible for any errors that may still appear.

For over fifty years now, the American legal and financial communities have experienced the application and elaboration of a concept of securities regulation known as "the disclosure philosophy."[1] Its legal antecedants were both ancient and respectable. For instance, partners, among themselves, and agents, to their principals, have long been required to make full disclosure of significant information relevant to the partnership or the agency. And a trustee of an express trust can deal only with the *cestui que trust* after making full disclosure of all information relevant to the transaction.

Nineteenth-century general incorporation acts required corporations, as a condition for their existence, to disclose in their article of

23

incorporation such matters as the number of shares the company would be authorized to issue, the par value of shares, and a variety of other matters. These corporations were also generally required by statute to "keep books and records" and to display them on occasion to shareholders. There is a relatively small amount of litigation in the corporate field involving shareholder efforts to secure this kind of information, though it is what federal laws seem to assume was most lacking. Oddly the courts still have a significant number of cases in which someone (usually involved in a control fight) is seeking the shareholder list.[2] But even with the shareholder demand for that information quite evident, the federal laws have offered no significant assistance.

Each of the early forms of required disclosure was generally aimed at some narrow, finely focused interest the law sought to protect. Legal enforcement of these rights to information was normally after the fact of nondisclosure, with the court granting an injunction or damages for the failure of a defandant to perform his duty properly. The costs of conforming to these older disclosure prescriptions were generally quite small and the law fairly easily understood. More important, these rules did not require an administrative organization to force disclosure in advance of a request for it.[3]

This era of relative laissez-faire in the market for information about stocks ended abruptly with the federal Securities Act of 1933. The process of interment continued with the Securities Exchange Act of 1934 and goes on to this day with a constant flow of new rules and regulations from the Securities and Exchange Commission.

To economists there is still considerable doubt, and little hard evidence, on the question of whether the amount of disclosure in securities matters became more or less optimal after these laws. The bulk of the evidence usually marshaled against the pre-1933 system is the testimony and documentation produced at the Senate hearings held before adoption of the acts.[4]

Those famous Pecora Hearings, filling eleven thick volumes, are almost exclusively anecdotal and impressionistic. They were largely what lawyers refer to as a "parade of horribles," tales of fraud, manipulation, and embezzlement—some real, some not—occurring in financial markets during the late 1920s. The hearings were carefully designed and professionally staged to create public mistrust in our financial institutions and to pave the way for the adoption of extensive securities regulation.

These hearings created a whole set of unproved popular beliefs about the stock market, including the notion that insider trading was

fraudulent and harmful to the small investors.[5]
We have had little careful investigation of
whether this belief ever had a significant basis in
fact. My own impression is that we have probably been fighting an illusion. It is certainly
doubtful, at the least, that the decade of the
1920s provided a greater proportion of securities
frauds than we have witnessed in recent years.[6]
Matters like *National Student Marketing*[7] and
Equity Funding[8] were not mere technical violations of the securities laws. They represented
the very kind of fraud that full-disclosure laws
were designed to dispel. This is suggestive, at
least, that a straightforward criminal enforcement program against fraud may have been more
appropriate and less costly than has the so-called
disclosure approach.

Much of the evidence adduced in the Pecora
Hearings related to insider trading in the stock
market, particularly the variety that was
formerly managed through the instrumentality
of a stock pool. Oddly, however, in spite of
what the public was led to believe, this insider
behavior was considered neither fraudulent nor
criminal prior to the Securities Exchange Act of
1934. The operation of trading pools was regularly reported in the financial press of time, but
that practice was outlawed explicitly in the
Exchange Act. Insider trading, on the other
hand, apart from the rather mild restrictions of

Section 16(b) of the 1934 Act, was not made generally illegal before the decision in the *Texas Gulf Sulphur* case[9] in 1968.

What little careful evidence we have about pre-1933 stock market behavior strongly suggests that there were no significant fraud problems in the market. George Benston has examined the incidence of fraud in accounting disclosures prior to 1934 and found it to have been almost negligible.[10] Professor Benston also found that the stock market prior to 1933 was very "efficient" in the sense of rapidly and correctly integrating new information into stock prices. The most important implications of this finding are that stock market pricing was probably honest and not manipulated in any significant degree and that the amount of disclosure was adequate to the market's observed demand and perhaps optimal.

Professor Benston has offered us one other interesting tidbit from the 1920s as well. Over half the companies listed on the New York Stock Exchange already disclosed the most significant financial information that was subsequently required to be disclosed by all companies subject to the Exchange Act. This strongly suggests that a market for information was functioning rather effectively without any governmental compulsion. The fact that more than half of the largest companies in the country were offering rather full periodic disclosure to the public was surely known to shareholders in the companies not disclosing. Yet no one has offered any evidence that shareholders in the nondisclosing companies were making lower rates of return than those in the disclosing companies. In fact, Benston suggests that the opposite was probably true.

It is only logical to conclude, therefore, that there were competitive reasons why some firms did and others did not engage voluntarily in this disclosure. True, this evidence may not be sufficient on which to base a final judgment about the initial or subsequent need for disclosure laws.[11] But we may certainly question the intellectual legitimacy of the birth of these laws.

I

Disclosure Under the Securities Act of 1933

Advocates of disclosure-type securities laws have long claimed that, like income tax and antitrust laws, disclosure does not interfere with legitimate business decisions. Disclosure is said, like antitrust, to make the market function

more, not less, effectively. And one of the
strongest defenses for disclosure laws was that
they did not require an inefficient bureaucracy
to pass on the merits of securities. We do not
hear that as much any more, but to this day the
phrase "merit regulation" has a bad connotation
to old hands at the SEC.

In fact, however, the argument that required disclosure is generally nonregulatory is as
mythical in the securities field as the analogous
arguments offered for antitrust laws or an income tax. For both theoretical and practical
reasons, disclosure laws necessarily force be-
haivor that differs substantially from what
would occur in the absence of the disclosure
rules, thus causing the same distortions in allocational and welfare efficency that occur with
direct, public utility-type regulations or the sort
we find with state Blue Sky laws.[12]

The disclosure and merit concepts overlap
when, in spite of the full listing of all the report-
able risk factors affecting a corporation's future
(including even the insolvency of the corporations), the Commission staff concludes that "the
offering might not result in the required 'bona-
fide distribution' to the public."[13] This, of
course, is a fiction, and the Commission is
simply refusing to allow individuals voluntarily
to assume a substantial but overt risk in an investment, the very essence of merit regulation.

The practice is generally thought to have increased in recent years.

Another method of regulation behavior under the guise of requiring disclosure occurs when a prospectus must state that the company has made a certain undertaking, which in fact the company would not have done were it not for this "disclosure."[14] Requiring the statement is thus tantamount to adopting a rule having the same import as the required statement, though the SEC may have no authority to make such a direct order.

For instance, registration statements, to achieve acceleration, must state certain restrictions on corporate indemnification of officers and directors for violations of securities laws, even though such a provision would not otherwise have been adopted.[15] But in the absence of this provision, the Commission staff will simply not permit the issue to be sold. Thus, by the requirement of a particular statement, the SEC can make any new legal rule it likes. The practice is so questionable, however, that the Commission has thus far used it sparingly.

Somewhat similarly, the SEC has ruled that financial disclosures not in accord with "generally accepted accounting standards" do not constitute full disclosure, no matter how inappropriate the generally accepted standard may be or how clearly explained the alternative approach.[16]

But the more significant economic effects of disclosure laws comes about in a more subtle way. There are barriers to competition inherent in any scheme that imposes substantially identical regulations on all firms in an industry regardless of differences in the firms' size or their modes of behavior, though these barriers may not be unwelcome to firms already well established in an industry.

William Hawley's important work, *The New Deal and the Problem of Monopoly,* [17] provided us with case histories of every federal regulatory scheme adopted during the period known as the New Deal. The picture portrayed is overwhelmingly one of private industry attempting through public means to avoid interfirm competition. With one exception I shall examine in a moment, the author concluded that regulation resulted because of strong political pressures from the leading firms in the industry or at least came with their strong approval.

This should come as no great surprise. The forces of competition, as Joseph Schumpeter so elegantly explained, are powerful, destructive, and unnerving. It is not surprising then that businessmen, laborers, farmers, teachers, and anyone else who can, should be willing to expend resources to protect themselves from these personal costs. Economists may think of this simply as another form of risk aversion, but that term is really too bland and moderate to convey the whole idea of purchasing protection from competition in the political marketplace.

But if these personal costs of competition were not present and people were not risk averse, we should still anticipate that some resources would be expended to secure protection from competition. This conclusion follows directly from the realization of two simple economic truths, one that monopoly profits are higher than competitive returns and the other that people prefer more to less of economic goods. To the extent that protection from competition can be purchased for a price less than the anticipated monopoly rents, we should expect that to occur. It is also clear that the government enjoys a substantial comparative advantage over the private sector in producing this service and that there are substantial economies of scale. There are also enormous external costs to the citizenry associated with this political market system, which, like a few private market externalities, may be impossible to internalize.

Oddly, the one New Deal regulatory scheme that Hawley does not fit into this pattern was that for the securities industry. This is more than passing strange. It suggests, first, that the interests of investment bankers in avoiding competition was somehow less than that of oil companies, radio stations, and truckers. Or it suggests that, even if they were as interested, they did not have as able lobbyists or lawyers working for them as the other industries did. But neither of these suppositions is likely to be correct, and I can only conclude that Hawley, like Homer, nodded. In his coverage of the SEC's origins, Hawley probably relied on popular secondary sources that took the politicians and the businessmen at their word. [18]

While we have little direct evidence to contradict Professor Hawley's somewhat unexpected exclusion of the underwriting industry from the pattern found universally by him and others elsewhere, there is at least circumstantial evidence to the contrary. Ironically, not the least of this circumstantial evidence is the fact that disclosure was adopted as the principal mode of regulation of the sale of new issues of securities.

Joseph Schumpeter confirmed about business what Shakespeare had earlier proclaimed for swordsmen, that the leading firm in any industry does not really have much to fear from other firms well established in the industry. They may shave price by pennies or cut costs slightly in an effort to make a better bottom-line showing at the end of the year, but they rarely threaten each other's very being. Rather it is the unorthodox, non-traditional entrant in an in-

dustry, or even the firm on the verge of bankruptcy, that is apt to be the shaker and mover,
the creative destroyer who unsettles otherwise
complacement modes of operation.[19]

And even if Schumpeter is often more dramatic than Shakespeare, we may still note that
the last entrant into an industry, or the not-
quite-surviving firm, often has to cut price or
assume higher costs simply to become established. Such actions occur at the expense of
firms presently assumed to be in competitive
equilibrium. Manifestly, this becomes more
serious if there is a significant decline in demand
for the industry's services, as certainly occurred
in the securities industry after October 1929.

There is some evidence that the securities
industry in the period between 1929 and 1933
made a number of private efforts to curtail in-
tensive competition.[20] Various associations of
firms were formed, and attempts were made to
enforce "canons of ethics" for their members.
But, of course, the more these "ethical" firms
agreed not to compete or interfere with established relationships between corporations and
underwriters, the more firms not abiding by
these prohibitions prospered.[21]

Then along came the New Deal, and the
man whom Wall Street claimed to hate most
offered the first really effective chance to over-
come the industry's own depression. The mode

of restriction on competition would, of course, have to "look right" to the public if the politicians were to risk pressing it, and in practice this meant that they had to align themselves with the "ethical" firms in the industry.[22] The trick, of course, was to find a regulatory device that would add relatively higher costs, because of comparative disadvantages, to those new or less efficient firms that cut prices while still giving the appearance of protecting the public.

If we look, then, for practices that distinguished leading underwriting houses from their "less ethical," more unsavory competitors, a strange fact emerges. One difference in their activities related to the degree and quality of the public disclosure made by these firms about the stocks they underwrote.[23] A prospectus prepared by a leading Wall Street house in 1928 could, with really insignificant differences in financial disclosures, obtain a clearance from the Corporate Finance Division of the SEC today.[24] But many firms flourished, or at least survived, by not marketing such "high-quality" stocks to their customers.

This similarlity between the requirements of the Securities Act of 1933 and the operations manuals of leading Wall Street houses of the time may have been coincidental and unintended. But a more likely explanation is that the industry leaders succeeded in channeling

Roosevelt's penchant for regulation into a valuable competitive advantage. The ensuing increase in relative costs weakened whatever comparative advantage sharply competing firms previously enjoyed in offering a different quality of service to their customers. Ultimately, shareholders in all companies using underwriters' services must have lost something by this shift away from competitive efficiency.

It should be possible to gain some probative evidence fo the theory just suggested. It should be possible to see whether, after the 1933 Act was adopted, the rate of return on invested capital for the underwriting firms already encouraging full disclosure by their customers went up significantly in comparison to those not previously doing so. And it would be interesting to see which underwriting firms tended to go into bankruptcy after the adoption of the Act. The SEC presumably has data on both these points, though there is a problem of multi-colinearity with these data since the firms shown to be losing may have been the same ones that would decline in a business downturn anyway. There is, however, no necessary reason why that should be so.

*   *   *

Assuming for the moment that a pure disclosure system of regulation is feasible, we begin our analysis by noting that certain information that would otherwise pose real costs to procure must be made available at approximately zero cost to the public. We may assume that this information has negative value, zero value, or positive value, but that in every case the process of disclosing is costly. Thus even though a given bit of information has positive economic value to its users, transactions costs necessary to communicate the information may still be greater than that value.

That most information required in a registration statement under the 1933 Act has zero value to prospective share purchasers, the intended beneficiaries, should come as no surprise.[25] Most of the information required to appear in prospectuses or S-1 registration statements is about facts that occurred long ago. It can be assumed already to have fully influenced the price of the company's outstanding stock or the stock being registered.[26]

In fact the S-1 registration was not designed for current disclosure purposes. As we shall see, the periodic reporting requirements and later Rule 10b-5 were designed to serve the purpose of forcing the disclosure of "new" news. The 1933 Act rather was designed principally to prevent false information from being used to hike the price of new issues.[27] Both the accounting rules and the particular disclosure requirements of the SEC developed with that particular attitude in mind.

This is not to suggest that Securities Act disclosures serve no purpose. At least three come to mind. First, the SEC is provided with an enormously powerful "enforcement" device. Delays in stock issues and huge monetary liabilities are among the more draconian penalties a company can suffer if it does not comply with the wishes of the Commission's enforcement staff. Probably no law-enforcement group in our legal system has the incredible threat power of the SEC and uses it so often.

Next the disclosure in an S-1 registration statement can be a tremendous boon to competitors. They, after all, are not particularly interested in whether information is reflected accurately in a competitor's stock. They are interested in the information itself. Probably the bulk of inquiries about filings come from competitors of the filing companies. There is no easy way to gauge the costs of this anticompetitive practice, but it may be significant.

A final group benefiting from the Securities Act disclosures are securities analysts. The whole SEC apparatus seems almost an ideal subsidy to that group. A cheap, available library of data, organized and filed, provides information on numerous companies for these analysts. Arguably, this is what the laws were designed to do, but if that is so, the intention seems misplaced. The subsidy is probably realized mainly by the analysts themselves, since the public would realize its information benefit even if the analysts' information costs were higher and if every analyst did not have all this information freely available. As Harold Demsetz has pointed out, forcing the subsidization of efforts that would in all probability be adequately funded privately does not seem like desirable government policy.[28]

Information can have negative value when reliance upon it imposes costs on those who believe it, as when the disclosure does not accurately communicate a significant underlying reality.

Historically, the most common form of required misinformation was financial information subject to the SEC's conservative accounting rules. Until quite recently, this approach precluded carrying assets on a balance sheet or in the inventory section of an income statement at a value higher than the cost, even though inflation may have made that figure meaningless and caused considerable overstatement of accounting income and possibly overvaluation of stocks. The SEC's rule precluding earnings projections also disadvantaged anyone relying solely on the official disclosures, though this one was recently relaxed.[29]

In recent years important spokesmen in the securities field, both professional and academic, have realized the costs of these conservative SEC accounting rules. In particular, former SEC Chairman William Casey[30] and Professor Homer Kripke[31] have urged their repeal or correction, as have such less sympathetic critics of the SEC as Professor Benston[32] and myself.[33] The Commission now appears on the verge of allowing more accurate financial reporting for companies with established financial records, but not for start-up companies.[34]

While there is no obvious economic justification for requiring the disclosure of information that has either negative or zero value, there may be positive benefits from the disclosure of information with a market value in excess of transactions costs. It has long been dogma in the securities regulation field that disclosure is desirable primarily because it will prevent fraud and deception, though scant economic justification has been offered in support of this notion. Still the main corpus of economic theory has long contained a doctrine seemingly tailor-made for justifying the required disclosure of valuable information.[35]

The doctrine of "public goods" defines a category of economic goods that can be consumed or enjoyed by one individual without

diminishing the simultaneous or subsequent enjoyment of the same economic good by others.
The classic illustration of this is radio or television broadcasting, the enjoyment of which by
one person in no way interferes with the full
enjoyment of it by others. Since this is so, many
economists argue that a user charge for goods
with this characteristic is necessarily suboptimal.
The welfare of an additional consumer of the
good can be increased by allowing him to have it
at no charge, while the benefit to no one else is
diminished thereby. Thus, under the conventional Pareto welfare economics approach, un-
less the goods are made freely available, the
good will be underconsumed and total social
welfare will be less than would otherwise be the
case. Certainly information of the kind found in
a prospectus seems to have these characteristics
and therefore would be underutilized by the
consuming public if a charge were made for it.

But there would seem to be several errors in
this argument. The first is that, while the public
goods argument for the free distribution of the
economic good is correct as a matter of allocational efficiency, it is incorrect as a matter of
productive efficiency. Though there may seem
to be Paretian savings in allowing additional persons to use the information without charge, we
would be left with a fundamental problem of
production incentives. If the producer of an

economic good is not allowed to obtain at least a market rate of return for his efforts and resources, he will have no incentive to produce the good.

On the other hand, it could still be argued that securities registration laws push disclosure closer to the Pareto optimal level since an issuer must disclose the "correct" amount of information or suffer the civil and criminal penalties provided by the securities laws. This might seem to take care of the incentive point, but a problem remains of determining which information should be produced and disclosed and the correct level of punishment for failure to disclose. The burden of making those decisions has simply been shifted from the private sector to the public one, though the record of the SEC in this regard is not encouraging.

There is still another reason why the conventional public goods argument does not fit financial information. The traditional argument, as mentioned, is based on the assumption that the usefulness of an economic good by one individual is not impaired through its use by another. Oddly, however, in the case of stock market information this is so only in one limiting circumstance. The economic value of a specific bit of information is rapidly exploited in the securities market by traders with that information. It will *not* have the same value to subsequent recipients of the information, since its total value will already have been realized in the market. In other words, the public goods characteristic of information is an illusion, since a second person cannot receive the same positive utility as the first without loss to the latter. The limiting case in which that is not true is the common but unimportant situation in which the information has zero market value.

Some might still defend the public goods argument on the ground that the Securities Act was designed to guarantee that *valuable* information must be distributed to all purchasers of a new issue before any one individual benefits in the market from the required information. Apart from the naïve factual assumption here, this view mistakes the public good argument for an equal access argument. Clearly equal access can be urged for many resources that have none of the characteristics of public goods, but the argument is merely one for reallocation of wealth on equity grounds. It has nothing to do with public goods.

*   *   *

A surprising number of truly fundamental questions about the Securities Act have received little or no analysis, even though a negative answer to any of them should dispel the high regard with which this law is popularly held. For instance, there is the question of whether 1933 Act required disclosure ever contained significantly valuable information for those to whom it is ostensibly addressed, or whether it can.

It is constructive to hear what leading practitioners and legal scholars in the field have commented on this point. A recent article by a leading securities lawyer, Carl W. Schneider, commented that "the SEC filings generally have an artificial or unreal quality. They purport to be full disclosure documents but, as a matter of convention, they exclude important types of information investors consider relevant, and stress much information investors consider irrelevant or relatively unimportant."[36]

Mr. Schneider quotes a U.S. district court judge: "In the face of such obfuscatory tactics the common or even the moderately well-informed investor is almost as much at the mercy of the issuer as was his pre-SEC parent. He cannot by reading the prospectus discern the merit of the offering." And Professor Homer Kripke has stated that he has "reluctantly come to the conclusion that the Securities Act of 1933 is not operating as it should, that the prospectus has become a routine, meaningless document which does not serve its purpose. . . . The real problem with the statutory prospectus is not that it is unreadable, but that it is unread. It is unread because it does not contain the information which the investors consider crucial to the investment decision."

These quotes—and hundreds more like them could easily be found[37]—all seem to contain a subtle implication that more could be done if the SEC had only been smarter or perhaps more diligent in designing the new-issue disclosure requirements. The individuals quoted never seem to ask why the Commission did not in fact require more helpful disclosure, or whether that was feasible at all. It is just assumed that the Commission could have done a better job.

It would seem, however, that there are good reasons why the SEC has followed the course that it has. Messrs. Schneider and Kripke complain that the SEC has taken too "conservative" an approach to disclosure, that it has required the disclosure only of actual past events, so-called hard facts, and has rejected attempts to predict the future.[38]

And yet it takes little consideration of the overall issue to realize that administrators feel an almost desperate need for objective criteria on which to base their disclosure rulings. Otherwise, they rapidly become enmeshed in a morass of conjecture and uncertainty that may interfere with the appearance of doing a fair and honest job. That appearance is probably more important to most regulators than are the economic interests of the public.[39]

But the administrators are not completely in control of the move to change. When legal writers of the stature of Carl Schneider and Homer Kripke point out actual faults in the present system, the courts, who no longer play a passive role in this process, will push the Commission, case by case, toward change. And it does not concern the judiciary, if they notice at all, that almost every change increases the total social costs of the regulatory scheme.[40]

Thus, in the last couple of years interest has been sparked in allowing, or even requiring, earnings projections in SEC filings. The problems are formidable. Projections cannot be presented simply as facts about the future. To be meaningful, the basis for the projection must be explained, as well as the techniques used in making projections, the reliability of experts who may have participated in the process, and a host of other "protective" requirements.[41] The inherent uncertainty about disclosing such information will be further aggravated by the danger of large civil liabilities if events develop in an unforeseen fashion. Making projections convey valuable information with a high degree of built-in reliability may make the problem of resolving conflicts in accounting standards look simple by comparison.

Our legal process, or perhaps we should call it our lawyering process, will inevitably develop protective devices and boilerplate language, just as it already has, so that the prospectus will still be "a routine, meaningless document which does not serve its purpose." The only safe prediction is that out of that morass will develop more unforeseen and unforeseeable problems requiring still additional regulations, disclosure, and work for the bar.

*   *   *

Presumably most regulatory and information-disclosure costs of a Securities Act registration can be avoided by using some form of private placement. Economic theory would have suggested then that the 1933 Act would have caused a relative shift from the use of the public issue device to private placements. In fact we have some quite strong empirical evidence to substantiate that hypothesis. Avery Cohen has noted that "In the thirty-four years from 1900 to 1934, about 3 percent of all corporate debt cash offerings, or approximately $1 billion were directly [privately] placed. However, in the ensuing thirty-one years, from 1935 to 1965, 46 percent, or $85 billion, were directly placed." [42] Some question of causation still remains, but George Benston, in an ingenious test of this question, concluded that the degree to which SEC requirements would cause misinformation in a given industry correlated very highly with the use of private placements as opposed to public issues. As mentioned earlier, these costs in the form of required misinformation may be the most important disclosure costs, since the information reported probably has no significant positive market value.

In this last respect the SEC's proposed new Rule 146 will apparently reduce some of the relative cost advantage previously enjoyed for private placements, not by decreasing the costs of public issues, but by increasing the costs of private placements.[43] However, if it is the misinformation in accounting data that has caused most of the shift to private placements, the new rule may be of small consequence. This is so since presumably the financial intermediaries who provided most of the private financing will be sophisticated enough to avoid being misled by these disclosures. On the other hand, it will be interesting to see whether that is in fact the case and, if not, whether the result will be more public offerings or simply fewer newer issues of any kind. The full implications of these findings are considerable, though the SEC has shown no interest in pursuing the inquiry.

There are anticompetitive implications to registration costs as well. Since there are clear economies of scale involved in selling shares of stock, the registration system operates as a regressive tax based on the size of the issue and presumably, therefore, the issuer. Public capital markets are made relatively less accessible to the small firms that would like to enter an industry or expand their present operations than they are for the large established firms in the same fields.

The disclosure requirements themselves are often apt to prove more onerous for new, small companies, than for large, established ones. Special disclosures for high-risk ventures, unavailability of earlier, audited financials; and illegality of earnings projections for companies without "track records" all illustrate this perverse discrimination—a pattern, incidentally, alleged to carry over into state Blue Sky regulation. According to Professor James Mofsky,[44] these laws have made it all but impossible for the small promoter to have access to public capital markets, the one source that might otherwise be tapped without the almost certain loss of entrepreneurial control.

But the costs are not visited exclusively on actual or would-be securities issuers. Some of these costs must be shifted to investors themselves, and indeed these costs might even be greater than any benefits derived from the same regulation.

To the extent that a given bit of information required to be disclosed has positive value, the risk of investment in the security under registration is ipso facto less than would otherwise be the case. Risk can simply be viewed as the converse of information.[45] Just as information is an economic good subject to the usual postulates about supply and demand, so risk is simply the other side of the coin. It is an economic bad, and people are on average risk averse. Thus any disclosure of valuable information lessens risk.

At this point many economists falter. Having seen any means for reducing risk in society, they show a tendency to accept the gain with no further concern. *Ceteris paribus,* the less risk the better. Unfortunately, however, the *cetera* do not remain *in paribus* when it comes to legislating risk out of existence. First, not everyone is actually risk averse. Las Vegas, the racetrack, sky jumping, and even the stock market testify to this simple truth. Furthermore, among those who are risk-averse, the degree of risk-aversion varies. Yet any system of complete disclosure must be an all-or-nothing system, one that cannot make sensitive responses to varying degrees of demand for the removal of risk (given costs) found in the market.

A system of full disclosure necessarily discriminates against those who are relatively less risk-averse and, *a fortiori,* against those who are not risk-averse at all. It was once conjectured that if we had had an SEC in the nineteenth century we should never have developed our domestic mining industry.[46] Unfortunately, we cannot know how many modern versions of the old, wildcat mining industry, with its frenzied, frontier, and probably fraud-ridden financing, the SEC has cost us. But many or few, no economic justification for this barrier to growth and market allocation of capital has appeared in the securities literature.

In 1964 George Stigler advanced the seemingly innocuous idea that thirty years of regulation should have provided sufficient data by which to judge the impact on investors of the Securities Act of 1933.[47] While some of his statistical or analytical techniques have been called into question, and certain errors were found by Professor Irwin Friend,[48] the basic point of Stigler's analysis—that shareholders and investors have not been benefited by this regulation—has not been refuted. Significant portions of the Stigler study remain uncontested, and significant portions of the Friend response display serious weaknesses.[49] For all the concern that economists proclaim for the inefficiency of capital markets,[50] as a profession they have not been particularly inclined to examine the effects of some of our most significant, if complex, capital market regulation.

One matter that has been noted in the literature is the fact that even our best financial reporting techniques can convey little valuable information about the future. Accounting, after all, developed to keep records of past transactions, and that simply is not the stuff of which stock prices are made. There are, to be sure, many cases in which the information conveyed does carry strong, reliable intimations about the future, given known exogenous changes. For instance, a large amount of long-term debt may portend lower relative costs in a period of extreme inflation. Generally, accounting as such can do little more than record the past, giving whatever limited information about the future this affords.

The SEC disclosure rules have long focused on traditional, conservative accounting methods, apparently in the mistaken belief that inflated book values were the source of considerable deception of the public.[51] It has taken the SEC nearly forty years to realize the futility of this approach.[52] That period, ironically, is longer than a broad-based, public stock market existed in the United States before we started regulating it. We never gave the market as much opportunity to correct itself we have allowed the political approach, though the latter is surely less responsive to demonstrated problems. It is hard not to believe that American investors have been ill-served by this regulatory apparatus.

Recently, in another departure from the disclosure philosophy, the Commission required that for certain high-risk issues, so-called hot issues, the registrants describe their "plan of operation" for the business.[53] This requirment, also found for raiders, but not for the incumbents, in tender offers and proxy fights, binds the registrant to follow the programs described in the filing. Any significant variance from the stated plan would require, at a minimum, the approval of the SEC, thus converting these small businesses into "wards" of the government. As Carl Schneider has pointed out, it is anomalous that this approach applies to "those companies which, as a class, would probably find it the hardest to develop reliable predictions, start-up enterprises filing a first registration statement." It may be anomalous, but unfortunately it is not inconsistent with the thrust of SEC policies.

A serious economic problem with the Securities Act of 1933 is its impact on market liquidity. It might be recalled that this Act applies only to "public issues" of securities. But ever since the Act was adopted, that concept has been troublesome, particularly as it related to sales of shares by "control persons," or shares originally taken in a private placement and in certain other situations generating "lettered" or restricted stock.

Two years ago the principal issue of reform facing the securities bar was the SEC's then newly proposed Rule 144 outlining the narrowly constrained circumstances under which such shares could be sold in the market without a registration. Rule 144 generally allows owners of restricted shares to sell only a tiny fraction of their holdings every six months. While it was advanced as a "clarification" of law in the area, it has occasioned more uncertainty, comment, and "new law" than any provision of recent memory.

The extraordinary interest in this provision and the incredible amount of writing and speaking about Rule 144 since its adoption strongly suggest that the administrative costs of registration are playing a significant role in the securities law area. Certainly what we have seen are not the wild clamorings of would-be confidence artists trying to gain licenses to defraud and deceive the public. And yet, for all of this, there has never been a single study of the economic impact of restricting the right of certain holders to sell shares.

But we can deduce some of these consequences. In the first place, restricting the sale of large amounts of securities, or substantially raising the cost of selling them, affects the efficiency with which capital markets can function. This is so, first, because the rule affects the supply of securities available in the market and therefore the relative price of the shares. This is probably not too significant because of the extremely high cross-elasticity of demand for shares with similar risk values. Still, incredible as it sounds, the SEC does not even keep systematic data on the total amount or number of shares so restricted, and in the aggregate, within particular risk categories, the figures might indeed be significant.

The restriction may also seriously inhibit the market's function of integrating new or corrective information into share prices. Holders of restricted shares may generally be the most knowledgeable traders and arguably those we should least want to preclude from the market. Again, however, the matter may be of little moment, since somehow information will out. But again, there is no data on the subject and apparently no concern about it. As far as I am aware, this is the first time this economic question has even been raised publicly.

II

Some Economic Issues Under the Securities Exchange Act of 1934

The Securities Exchange Act of 1934 was a patchwork bill designed to cover a variety of matters that could not be accomplished in the few months taken for drafting, hearings, and adoption of the 1933 Act. A few of the Exchange Act's provisions more or less followed the disclosure philosophy, though that idea was not paramount. As to matters of disclosure, the Act enabled the newly created Securities and Exchange Commission to require periodic disclosure filings, to establish proxy regulations, and to issue rules against fraud; and it contained a rather mild, part-disclosure, form of regulation of insider trading.

The only specific disclosure requirement directly affecting securities trading stated in the original Exchange Act is the requirement of Section 16(a) that purchases and sales of securities by "statutory insiders" be reported. Unlike Commission-promulgated Rule 10b-5,[54] which by its terms applies to "anyone," Section 16(a) affected only officers, directors, and holders of more than 10 percent of a class of equity securities of a company subject to the Act. Prior to

1964 this was only companies listed on a registered stock exchange. After 1964 this became
any corporation with more than 500 shareholders of $1 million in assets.

Even this insider reporting requirement was
not intended to force disclosures useful in pricing securities. Rather, it was designed to help
enforce Section 16(b)'s aim of preventing insiders from utilizing unpublished information to
their own short-term trading profit. Section
16(b) required that profits realized by statutory
insiders from any combination of a purchase and
a sale of a stock within a six-month period be
turned over to the corporation.

There are various ways an insider can avoid
the reach of this provision. The simplest, of
course, is to hold the stock for six months. And
since the holding period for federal capital gains
tax treatment is also six months, it is doubtful
that Section 16(b) significantly reduces the
amount of informed trading that insiders would
do in its absence.

In 1967 James Lorie and Victor Niederhoffer studied the insider reports filed with the
Commission under Section 16(a).[55] They discovered that even though insiders realized a
higher-than-market rate of return on their reported transactions, their trades did not exhaust
the economic value of their information. Lorie
and Niederhoffer concluded that anyone who

quickly followed 16(a) reports in his own trading would also realize above-average returns, though it was not clear that these would exist if full transactions costs were taken into account.

This finding by Lorie and Niederhoffer was surprising in some respects. In my 1966 book on insider trading, I had assumed that the disclosing of insider short-swing transactions would effectively prevent insiders from using information from their own companies. Thus, I anticipated that 16(a) filings would not disclose any valuable information. I had assumed that any valuable information would somehow be used to realize quick trading profits. But I had discounted much too strongly the attraction of buying and holding for a period in excess of six months.

But these transactions were probably the only ones Lorie and Niederhoffer were measuring, since any realized short-term profits would have resulted in liability. However, the Lorie and Niederhoffer data were all pre-*Texas Gulf Sulphur*,[56] and today we should anticipate a different result than they reached. Post-*Texas Gulf* it is no longer necessary both to buy and sell a security to be liable. Consequently, single insider transactions based on undisclosed information are less likely to occur today since they must be reported, and liability may ensure under Rule 10b-5 even if there is no actual realization of a trading profit. My original supposition about the information that would show up in 16(a) filings, though wrong at the time, is probably correct today.[57]

For many years the most extensive reporting requirements under the 1934 Act were the SEC's proxy rules. At least prior to 1964 the amount of disclosure required under the SEC's lengthy proxy rules was second only to that required for a 1933 Act registration. That disclosure, however, always tended to relate to the subject up for shareholders' voting, either in an election of directors or on approval of some corporate action. Rarely was much financial disclosure made in the proxy statement.

However, the proxy disclosures had other advantages. They had to be mailed directly to shareholders of the companies subject to the proxy rules. And though, early on, this occurred only if the company actually solicited proxies, eventually either a proxy statement or its equivalent in an annual report had to be mailed to every shareholder. This meant that whatever information they did contain was sent to shareholders once every year, whereas a prospectus was only made available to offerees in the rare event that a company had a public offering.

While the proxy rules have been the subject of some important and some bizarre cases dealing with financial disclosure,[58] that has never been the real hallmark of this particular disclosure development. Rather the proxy rules developed because of a belief in the 1930s and 1940s that American publicly held corporations should be more democratically run. And democracy, as Berle and Means maintained in their influential book, *The Modern Corporation and Private Property* in 1933, functions efficiently only if the voters are well informed. This political notion implied the necessity for very detailed disclosure of a certain kind, since in theory the shareholders were supposed to evaluate and elect the best qualified managers for their corporations.

This theory sounds terribly naive to us today, and somewhere along the way, either sophistication or cynicism prevailed. Among securities lawyers today only the uninitiated take the idea of shareholder democracy seriously. The proxy solicitation system, or its non-proxy variant, has now become a straightforward disclosure device with no one very concerned one way or the other about the concept of democracy.[59]

This kind of fundamental change in the purpose to be served by a given law characterizes many administrative developments. This process not only fails to generate empirical testing of the effectiveness or desirability of the developing rules by those responsible for the changes, it is

apparently hostile to such attempts. Recently
Professor George Benston developed and
published some extremely careful and useful
tests of the effects on investors' returns of the
periodic filings of financial data that the SEC
had required from its inception.[60] These included the 8K monthly reports, 9K (now 10Q)
quarterly reports, and the 10K annual reports,
the last one of the most extensive financial
filings required by the SEC. The proxy rules as
such were not examined, but the implications
for that variant on periodic reporting were clear.

Commissioner A. A. Sommer, Jr., perhaps
the most highly respected securities lawyer ever
to sit on the Commission, took Benston to task
for ignoring the "salutory influence of the proxy
rules," which, he asserted, afforded shareholders
"important information" concerning their corporations.[61] But he offered no data or evidence
by which the most open-minded person in the
world could judge the validity of this assertion,
nor did he explain the lack of success Benston
noted for the periodic disclosures studied. Moreover, Sommer flatly criticized Benston and other
economists who attempt to "compress the com-
plexity of our securities markets and the multi-
tude of investor decisions into [horribly compli-
cated] formulae. . . ." Presumably, bland as-
sertions of unsupported conclusions are to be
preferred to "extensive statistical analysis" and

"horribly complicated formulae." That may be a correct reading of SEC legal history, even if it is not terribly satisfying methodologically.

Since the SEC had early called the failure to disclose material information a "principal contributing factor" to the success of the "manipulation by massive pool operations" in over 100 stocks during 1929, Benston first examined the effects of pool operations in each of those more than 100 stocks. This had never been done before. Strikingly, he discovered that the percentage of companies subject to pool operations and disclosing their sales and cost of goods sold was almost exactly the same as the percentage of companies subject to pools and not making such disclosure! Thus pool operations, whether successful or not, appear to have been unrelated to the disclosure practices of the companies involved.

Benston examined in *Moody's* the financial reports of corporations whose shares were traded on the New York Stock Exchange. He found that prior to the enactment of the disclosure requirements of the 1934 Act all of the corporations had published financial statements audited by CPAs. However, some 38 percent did not disclose sales, the most significant item whose disclosure was required by the SEC. Benston then reasoned that if the SEC-required disclosure provided investors with valuable information, there should have been greater revaluation on the shares of those corporations that were newly required to disclose sales compared with those already making such disclosure. Benston could find no such revaluation. Nor did he find greater changes in the measured riskiness of the shares of the newly disclosing corporations.

Benston, also for the first time, studied the question of whether the periodic disclosure requirements can provide information to investors in time to be of significant value. If this information is valuable and is reaching investors in time to be useful, he reasoned, it should have an impact on market price in the period when the (assumed) previously unanticipated information becomes publicly available.[62] On average, he found a 100 percent unexpected increase (or decrease) in the rate of change of income is associated with a mere 2 percent increase (or decrease) in the rate of change of stock prices in the month of announcement. The statistical correlation between these two rates of change is extraordinarily small. And, anticipating the SEC's next line of defense, Benston found the same result when he tested for the argument that, even if periodic reports are not timely, the required disclosure provides confirmation of preliminary reports and press releases on which the market price may now be based.

Professor Benston also addressed what,

judged by the number of times one hears it, is clearly the SEC's favorite argument: without mandatory disclosure the public would lose confidence in the securities markets and refuse to invest in American industry. The argument has always had an implausible ring, since a larger percentage of the American population was directly involved in the stock market prior to 1929 than was for almost the next forty years. That is, more people had "confidence" in the stock market prior to the SEC than have subsequent to it. It is doubtful, moreover, that the 1929 crash changed human motivation for all time.

The SEC's argument rests on the totally unverified and even illogical notion that fraud and deception, not financial losses, drove the public out of the market after October 1929 and would do so again regardless of the returns shareholders make from stock investments. This is sheer self-serving puffery by the SEC. As Professor Benston points out, it is losses on stocks that reduce investor confidence, and periods of great losses have occurred both before and after the 1929 crash and the 1934 Act's adoption. The SEC's confidence argument has some of the characteristics of a confidence game.

It is true that, unlike the proxy rules, the periodic disclosures examined by Professor

Benston are not usually mailed directly to the shareholders. But it is unlikely that the real costs of the information are significantly higher when professional securities analysts examine the periodic filings at regional SEC offices and transmit only relevant information to clients. As Professor Kripke has long maintained,[63] information addressed to the more sophisticated group is likely to be the more helpful anyway. The information required by the more direct forms of disclosure laws almost certainly gets to the rank-and-file shareholder too late to contain any trading value.

In case this last statement still surprises anyone, we have the somewhat ironic admission of Commissioner Sommer that "everyone knows that the income per share in the Form 10-K of a reporting company does not strike the financial community like a thunderbolt when the Form is filed. It has become known weeks before—and when it did [sic] it impacted market prices if earnings reported contradicted expectations; this we know from everyday experience."[64]

The commissioner tried in the same speech to extricate himself from the startling implications of this admission by talking about "assuring the integrity" of earlier releases and the like. But the important fact remains that he clearly acknowledged what Beston and I and a few others have been saying for a long time, but which SEC insiders usually admit only in unguarded moments, that required disclosure serves no significant market function. The whole "disclosure philosophy" as a basis for securities regulation is close to being a fraud on the American investing public, providing unwarranted benefits to government officials, securities lawyers, accountants, financial analysts, and printers.

*   *   *

Actually, the conclusion reached by Professor Benston and admitted by Commissioner Sommer is perfectly consistent with the most significant findings of modern financial theory, namely, that stock price changes follow a random walk pattern and that the stock market is very efficient in accurately and speedily impacting or integrating the value of new information.[65] It would serve no purpose to summarize the vast literature on this subject here. The fundamental conclusions of this research have changed little in the fifteen years or so that it has been developing[66] or in the ten years since Professor Baumol's excellent summary in *The Stock Market and Economic Efficiency*.[67] It is sufficient for us merely to note that the support for these findings has been nearly unanimous, while few limitations on their usefulness have been noted.

Like so many advances in the field of economics science, neither the random-walk theory nor the efficient-market hypothesis developed with a view toward policy applications. Even today, when the literature on these subjects threatens to engulf the field of finance, few economists writing on the subject draw policy conclusions from their work. And when they do, the recommendation is typically timid and naive, like suggesting that the SEC do additional studies on the possibility that earlier reporting of insiders' trading would benefit interested investors.[68] And economists have shown no great enthusiasm for the furious and often acrimonious debate surrounding the question of insider trading. Yet both the random-walk hypothesis and the efficient-market theory have substantial and fundamental implications for SEC policies on insider trading and on the whole matter of disclosure.

Stated in terms familiar to financial analysts, the random-walk hypothesis means that nothing in the previous history of a stock's price movements gives information useful in predicting future price movements. In turn, this form of the random-walk hypothesis is consistent with a situation where any new development affecting the value of a company's shares is *instantaneously* integrated into the price of those shares. Otherwise the trading pattern generated by the trading on the new information would itself provide valuable trading information. [69] Thus, in the strong form, no one acquiring information after it was "known"[70] by anyone else could use it to realize greater-than-normal rates of return in the stock market. Ironically, however, strong-form-random-walk theorists consider the market to be "inefficient" if insider trading is present,[71] even though insider trading, as we shall see, may be one of the principal determinants of the efficient market.

In his review of the literature on this subject, Professor Eugene Fama has stated that "at the moment . . . corporate insiders and specialists are the only two groups whose monopolistic access to information has been documented." [72] Fama meant that certain members of these groups systematically make greater returns in the stock market than they would with a random or chance selection process, even though for other participants, given their preferred level of risk, no such returns are possible. These exceptions to the implications of the strong-form-random-walk theory are said by Fama to represent, at least to some extent, a failing in the strong form hypothesis and "an inefficiency" in the market. It should be noted, however, that this is not a claim that there are interdependencies in price changes, but rather a logical inference, or perhaps merely a definitional statement, about the fact of greater-than-market rates of return being systematically realized.

Certainly, the level of agreement among economists on these points gives confidence that the various studies of the random-walk and efficient-market hypotheses have been properly executed. But more might still be desired from the point of view of policy makers in the securities field. First, all the tests establishing the existence of a random walk have been empirical studies of various price changes in relation to specific forms of information. But we have been told little about how the random series is generated.[73] As we shall see, a direct test of that point may be impossible, and we may have to rely on logical inferences from negative tests.

Paul Samuelson has offered one logical explanation of why we should anticipate that stock prices would follow a random course.[74] Following his lead, we should first assume that the stock market is efficient in integrating new information correctly and quickly. If that is so, there is nothing left to influence present price changes except exogenous circumstances that presumably will occur at random intervals and with random intensities. Adding these two suppositions, the stock market can logically only reflect a random walk, though, as Samuelson reminds us, this does not in itself prove that actual competitive markets work well or that randomness of price change is desirable. That requires a different investigation.

Another theory,[75] which in some sense makes less heroic assumptions than Samuelson's, begins by viewing the market as being occupied by many people with no valuable information and by a few people who on occasions do have valuable information. At any given moment there would be numerous offers by uninformed traders to buy and to sell at almost every imaginable price. In the absence of some kind of information about market prices, any price asked by one of them that happened to coincide with a price bid by another would create a market transaction. The price changes would clearly be random and variances from the mean price great.

The organized stock market itself will provide a limitation on this pricing scheme.[76] This market will provide, at almost no cost, information about the prices at which other, presumably better informed, purchases or sales took place, and will to some extent, therefore, curtail the variances in price changes that might otherwise characterize this market. Moreover, specialists, block positioners, and market makers will utilize their knowledge of the various offers to buy or sell stocks (the orders in the "book") to keep price movements within additional limits. Finally, analysts and insiders who are confident of their evaluation of a company's stock will find it in their interest to engage in transactions tending to level what might still be rather large price fluctuations.[77]

Although the random-walk and efficient-market theories are now generally accepted, explanations of how or why these phenomena exist are less well developed in the literature. Nonetheless, some traders must have early (i.e., pre-SEC disclosure) access to information. This can be either because they "make" it, discover it, or receive it automatically because of their positions.

One can be said to make information if he procures a desirable contract, invents a new product, or otherwise develops a higher profit (or loss) potential for a company. This group would include the founders or promoters of new ventures as well. It does not follow that every maker of valuable new information will be able to exploit it in the market, but in many cases this will be so.

The principal "discoverers" of information are probably securities analysts, whether they ferret out their information by questioning executives, by analyzing published data, or by following up on tips from others, as happened in the notorious Equity Funding episode. Usually these "discoverers" of information will not come up with the "million-dollar find" that did occur with Equity Funding, but clearly returns to this effort are sufficient to provide gainful employment to a small army of these private investigators. That they perform a socially valuable function cannot be disputed, and the economic effects of penalizing an investigator for too much success, as the New York Stock Exchange seems bent on doing to Mr. Raymond Dirks, uncoverer of the Equity Funding scandal, should be manifest to anyone. The role of operators like Mr. Dirks in keeping the market as efficient as it is and inhibiting either artificially low or high prices from persisting should be clear to everyone concerned with public policy in this area. But apparently it is not.

Another group who "discover" information are specialists, block positioners, and market makers. This group "discovers" not fundamental information about the company but potential extreme variances in market prices. As described earlier, they perform the valuable task of preventing uninformed buyers and sellers from generating wildly gyrating prices. By thus reducing variances, they reduce the overall riskiness of market transactions. As we shall see below, however, there may be some monopoly rents involved in the provision of specialists' services that do not seem warranted.

Finally, we come to the group whose early access to information occasions the greatest dismay for regulators of securities markets and of community moral standards. I have reference, of course, to those individuals who, as a result of their professional positions, have early access to valuable information. They may be officers of companies, lawyers, accountants, bankers, secretaries, janitors, or what have you. I have been nearly alone in defending the right of these individuals to profit from their legally obtained information if they are not forbidden to do so by their own contractual arrangements. I have had a bit more company agreeing with me that policing this group may be impossible, or at least not worth the costs.[78] And finally, I suppose the number of supporters grows even larger when I state merely that this group, like the others mentioned above, serve the economically valuable purpose of causing the market to function efficiently.[79]

There are certain differences in the information marketing procedures of the various functionaries mentioned above. The specialists' behavior seems, aside from antitrust issues, to be perfectly legal and generally approved. Securities analysts are somewhat more suspect, and occasionally, as with Mr. Dirks, may even be penalized for their efforts. But the insiders, who probably do the most to keep the stock market efficient, must operate clandestinely and under a cloud of criminality and ignominy if they are caught. It is my guess now, as it was in 1966,[82] that they have developed numerous schemes, artifices, and devices to hide (sometimes perhaps even from their own conscious recognition) their market-correcting transactions.

But having declared their transactions illegal, we now cannot prove whether they effectively serve this purpose or not or how great the costs are for shifting their information to legitimate users (say overseas funds).[81] Presumably, however, the effect of the SEC's 10b-5 campaign, first publicized in *Texas Gulf Sulphur*, [82] has been to make the stock market somewhat less efficient than it was formerly. Black markets are not, after all, as efficient as free markets. Luckily, however, they are a lot more efficient than the controlled markets for which they substitute. We are still awaiting a decisive—or even an indecisive—test of the economic effects of that decision on the efficiency of the market.

*   *   *

It should be noted that the random-walk theory of the stock market is not the same as the famous Keynesian roulette wheel analogy. In a memorable error in his *General Theory of Money, Interest and Employment*, Keynes posited the arbitrariness of a stock's price at any given moment and advanced an ingenious copycat theory of why this would be true.[83] He argued that market participants in a search for information would behave like the entrants in a newspaper beauty contest based on the entrants' votes. Each would attempt to assess which contestant others would vote for, or, better, whom others thought others would vote for, and so forth. Thus, little attention would be given to an entrant's own beauty preference, and the outcome would bear little relationship to a true preference poll.

Professor William Baumol at one time seemed sympathetic to this view of stock market pricing.[84] He was struck by the apparently perverse facts that an increase in the supply of shares did not necessarily cause more shares to come onto the market at a higher price.[85] He was presumably referring to an existing, fixed supply of shares, since the available evidence suggests that this is not true for all companies within a given risk range so far as new issues are concerned. But it would appear that Baumol was not viewing the relevant commodity.

What is being bought and sold in the stock market is not, as he implied, exclusively the underlying investment security about which all information is known. Rather, exchanges more often take place because of differing expectations about the future prospects of the company. The parties, in effect, "bet" on their information. What we have is a market for "share" packages that tie together two commodities, a security and information, the values of which are related in a complex fashion. It was the effects of the market for information that Baumol was observing and not the effects of the market for investment securities alone. Viewed this way, as we shall see, the apparent perverseness of this market disappears, as does any support for Keynes' pricing view.

The production and the demand for information about a given stock is independent of the demand for the security itself. In order to market monopolized or previously unpublicized information (assume that it is good news), one can purchase securities in the market at the prevailing price. After the release of this information, the information as such will have zero market value, but the price of the shares will rise accordingly, and the informed purchaser of stock will in effect have "sold" his information.

The price of the security may have increased either because of the purchases of shares or because the information became known to those already holding shares who then raised their reservation price.[86] In my 1966 book I clearly overemphasized the former function and hypothesized that it was the actual purchase of the shares, not the disclosure of information, that makes a stock price appreciate.[87] After the purchases raised the price, disclosure would have a kind of ratchet effect and lock the value of the information into the security price. But if even an informed stock buyer tried before his information was disclosed, to sell stock that had appreciated because of purchases, his own sale would have reduced the price of the stock symmetrically.

The weakness in this view resulted from my failure adequately to incorporate the extremely high cross-elasticities of demand for individual stocks into the theory.[88] In fact, because of this factor, even relatively large purchases of a given stock may not cause the price to rise to the level indicated by the information motivating the purchases, thus occasioning the apparently perverse effect Baumol noticed.[89]

But while it is certainly possible for a stock price to change with little or no trading, it may also change because of trading pressures, since the cross-elasticities are never infinite. The determining factor is the relative influences of the demand to purchase shares and of the demand to hold them.

If traders gain information and seek to buy shares from holders who do not have the information, a large number of transactions may occur with little or no change in the quoted market price since there has been no change in the holders' reservation price.[90] On the other hand, whether the demand for shares goes up or not, if present holders of the shares get the information before other informed purchases begin, they will raise their reservation price and no shares may be traded at all. But it is impossible to say a priori in a given case which of these influences will predominate or to preclude a higher demand to purchase shares as at least one cause of the higher price.

This focus on the market for information as opposed to a market for stock viewed as a single commodity should be very helpful in developing desirable public policies in this area. For one thing, it points up quite clearly that "inside information" may be used frequently by present *holders* of stocks with no concern for the developing laws against insider trading under Rule 10-b. After all, it is very difficult to prove that a person benefited from undisclosed information when all he did was raise his reservation price and *not sell* at the old price. Yet it now seems apparent that this form of insider "trading" may be more common than the type in which a person seeks to *buy* shares. The economic effect, in any event, is the same, and the law looks a little bit, as Mr. Bumble would have it, like "a ass."

Furthermore, a focus on the information market allows us to view the matter of insider trading, not in terms of the morals of the stock market,[91] but rather in terms of the efficiency with which a market for information functions

and the extent to which information is used or
recognized as a valuable commodity in commercial dealings. And, as we shall see, this approach
may have some surprising implications for current debates not usually considered to be related
to the economics of information at all.

*   *   *

Economists have now shown that information of various kinds is integrated into a security's price before public announcement of the
information is made. For instance, in one of the
best-known studies, Fama, Fisher, Jensen, and
Roll[92] showed that a stock split usually signals
happier prospects for a company. They then
showed that this information had already been
reflected in the stock price by the time of the
stock split announcement. They concluded that
the stock market was efficient in terms of
reflecting new developments about a company.
However, as Professor Robert A. Schwartz
has pointed out,[93] this does not tell us how efficiently the market is operating. It only sets an
outer limit, the SEC-required disclosure date, to
the time period within which the information is
reflected in the price. Thus, studies like that of
Fama, Fisher, Jensen, and Roll only prove that
the market is more efficient than existing SEC
rules would seem to imply. And while that is

interesting and quite significant for present purposes, it would still be helpful to know, in some quantitative sense, just how efficient this market is in assimilating new information.

But this is a troublesome question. If we are to measure the speed with which the market assimilates a given piece of information, we must have some way of knowing when that "bit" of information comes into existence. And there's the rub. We cannot say that information about a stock dividend first exists on the day that the board of directors voted it. As a matter of fact, that particular procedure is in most cases a mere formality for rubber-stamping a decision made earlier.

Then when was the earlier decision made? Can we say that it was made at the time that some financial official within the corporation looked over various reports and concluded that he should recommend a stock dividend to the board? Clearly not, for his decision was significantly determined by the data that he examines, each bit of which in turn had its own multiple origins. Consequently, the "fact" of a certain unspecified probability that the stock dividend resolution would be adopted existed at the time certain bits of information about the company's affairs developed, and that would include numerous pieces of financial, economic, legal, business, or even political information.

So the more we seem to close in on this elusive point in time from which to measure the speed of the market assimilation process, the further we get from anything useful. The quest seems doomed to failure; there is no single piece of data which determines a specific outcome in this sense. A confluence of various pieces of data, all developing at different times, created a pressure that might ultimately move the company to declare a stock dividend. But usually there simply is no fixed point of time from which to measure objectively the average speed of the information dissemination process.

Furthermore, at every stage in this process we are talking about a probability continuum. Even a company on the verge of bankruptcy has some positive probability that it will in the future pass a stock dividend. And even a company whose board has adopted such a resolution does not have a 100 percent certainty that they will not be required by a court, the SEC, or the IRS to reverse that decision later.

None of this is meant to say that there are never specifically identifiable events that occur at a particular moment in time to which the stock market price reacts with a discernible degree of speed. However, these events are strangely difficult to identify and usually have such unique characteristics that they do not provide systematic data for careful analysis. They almost have to be of the so-called act of God variety, occurring without advance human planning or development, since that would lead us again through the endless chain of causation that so vexes this effort.

It is interesting to note that the law has had to struggle with a similar problem in determining when information subject to an insider trading violation is material. Economists may be surprised to learn that lawyers have refined this matter to a considerably greater extent than they have. In fact, they have reached the point where the ultimate argument is whether a given piece of information "would" influence a "reasonable investor" as opposed to whether it "might" influence such an investor.[94] To economists this may sound amusing, and it may appear that lawyers rush in where economists fear to tread.

On the other hand, lawyers rush in because a legal system must be able to resolve disputes even when scientific and objective measurement is lacking. The more important question is whether, given our lack of knowledge in an area, the issue should be addressed at all. And in answering that question our regulators and lawyers and judges have simply ignored the economic aspects that we can identify and understand.

There are actually some rather strong a priori reasons for believing that the market for information functions quite efficiently compared with other markets, even though we have no direct data on the question. First and foremost, the lure of tremendous gain is there to provide the motivating force required for any market to function. Though we have no clear estimates of the actual amounts involved, it would not be surprising if it were on the order of billions a year. The figure would include amounts involved in unanticipated changes in reported earnings, various changes in firms' competitive positions, inventions, political actions, and corrective moves by specialists and others to keep prices within appropriate trading ranges.

Equally important to consider is the ease with which a market for information operates. That is, the costs of transmitting, exchanging, and using information are generally quite low. While part of this assertion relates to the assumed inability of the SEC to effectively police its rules against insider trading, the point actually goes beyond that. It suggests that we should anticipate a very efficient stock market since, in the last analysis, inefficiency in that market would merely be reflective of high transactions costs.

Finally, perhaps a note should be added about the near impossibility of monopolizing the whole market for information in any significant sense. It is true that every "bit" of information is unique and that we can logically talk of a person "monopolizing" information. However, there could not be any significant restraint on the production of new information, and the cross-elasticity of demand for any bits of information must approach infinity. In other words, the market for information and consequently the stock market should be extremely efficient markets.

*   *   *

Various proposals for partly or fully integrating the various stock exchanges and markets into one single market have been much in the news of late. The concern that has led to the present dispute is the agreed presence of some monopoly influences in the New York Stock Exchange. At least since the SEC's Special Study in 1962, and quietly for many years before that, fixed commission rates on the Big Board have stuck in the throat of many champions of competitive markets.[95] The third market, it is generally assumed, developed in response to these cartel rates, and the whole debate about institutional membership, regional exchange practices, give-ups, unified tapes, a single exchange, negotiated rates, and other matters too could all be traced to this single concern.[96] But apparently no one has recognized that a monopoly return on information might be relevant to these disputes as well.

It has been clearly demonstrated by Niederhoffer and Osbourne[97] that specialists on the floor of the exchange make greater-than-market rates of return in their stock market dealings. As we have seen, they have access to valuable information that has not and, probably from its nature, cannot become generally known to the investing public. They have the monopoly accesss to the information about orders to buy and sell contained in their "book."

In standard economic theory, a monopolist's return will, to the extent allowed by transactions costs, be competed away in the marketplace. But these specialists' returns seem to have persisted at a high level over a considerable length of time, indicating that the transactions costs for displacing New York Stock Exchange specialists may be unusually high. This is most often the case, of course, if the monopoly position is protected by law, since then the transactions costs for competing away the monopoly profits in effect become infinite. But this does not seem to be the case with the New York Stock Exchange and its specialists. There were and are other functionaries willing and able to perform both the brokerage and the specialist's information functions at a lower return. All a competitor had to do was start a new exchange.

And that, of course, is exactly what the third market is.

Probably both of these monopoly services were significant contributing factors to the development of the third market, though most observers have assumed that the monopolistic powers of member firms in brokerage work was the total explanation. This probably was the primary cause, but the specialists' return was not insignificant, and, after all, the principal third-market participants were creating much of the market information that became of such value to specialists on the floor of the Exchange. Thus it should not have been surprising that these same traders should try to claim some of the value of this information for themselves. And even if brokerage fees had always been fully negotiated, there would still have been some reason for the development of a third market. The block positioner, it might be noted, is presumably competing only with the specialists' information function.

Much of the stance taken by the New York Stock Exchange in the current debate about rates, membership, and a unified market appears consistent and rational when viewed in this light. Thus, the Exchange seems to have accepted as a political reality that monopoly returns on the brokerage function must be forsaken. But if all stock transactions could be brought under the general surveillance of the New York Stock Exchange *and the functioning of its specialists*, at least those recipients of monopoly rents might still be protected. It should be equally clear why third-market activists like Weeden & Co. might still prefer not to settle for half a loaf. The concept of a market for information suggests that the various moves today toward any form of single unified stock exchange are probably ill-advised from a competitive point of view and that competition, both for brokerage services and for market information, should be encouraged.

* * *

I should like to turn now to a point alluded to earlier, that the stock market, viewed in part as a market for information, must contain incentives for the production of new information if it is to perform all of its market functions effectively. This point occasioned perhaps more concern—apoplexy might be the more accurate term—than any in my work on inisder trading, as I suggested that information was not an inappropriate medium of compensation for the performance of certain economic functions in large corporations.

Professor Jack Hirshliefer has pointed out, as have other critics of this part of my work, that if the "producer" of information is given the first, or monopolistic, crack at the market, he has as much incentive to produce bad news and sell short as he does to produce good news and purchase.[98] On balance, I think that this is incorrect, even though in my earlier work I conceded some merit to Section 16(c) of the Exchange Act, which forbids short sales by statutory insiders. But the question of motivation is not resolved by noting that profits can be made on bad news. By that logic no one should be paid a salary who can engage in any shirking on the job.

The ability to obtain benefits from bad news will simply be counted as part of the total compensation that may be realized by an individual in a given position. Preventing its occurrence requires the same kind of monitoring solution economic theory offers for other shirking costs.[99] Here the problem seems quite unsubstantial. Bad-news profits are neither the exclusive nor the main form of compensation an executive will be concerned to realize, and he will not prefer bad news if other forms of compensation are sufficient to determine the direction of his preference.

And clearly they are. Promotions, higher salaries, stock options, other job offers, and profit-sharing plans, for instance, should be sufficient generally to determine the quality of the

information any individual will prefer developing. If the various legal and market constraints
are operating efficiently, the intentional production of bad news should be a fairly rare occurrence. In any event, the opportunities to repeat
tend to disappear rapidly. The production of
good news, on the other hand, will be encouraged forever.

No system is without costs, to be sure, but
those who see the information-as-compensation
argument only in terms of its bad-news costs are
neglecting the more important part. At the
moment, at least, I can find little evidence or
theory strongly suggesting that in an unregulated
market for information there would be either an
"overproduction" problem[100] (as is sometimes
alleged for the patent system) or a perverse
incentive problem.

But there is another popular objection to
the compensation argument. It is that there is no
guarantee that the "information producer" will
also be the one to claim the stock market profits. That is, the benefits of trading on previously
undisclosed information may enure to the
"wrong" person, and thus insider trading would
not provide an efficient incentive system.

While we have no evidence either way on
this question, we might still inquire why, if certain information is truly valuable and that fact
can be recognized, the producer should allow

himself to be systematically exploited. Why should he continue to produce a valuable product for which he does not in some fashion recover the market value?

All that is required for this market to be in equilibrium is the common recognition that a particular position in a corporation or investment banking firm, or wherever, provides access to valuable information. Then, so long as competitors for these positions view the information as additional compensation for that position, they will presumably compete down the monetary component of the return to that position. So long as job markets are based on utility maximization rather than on purely monetary maximization,[101] they should operate as indicated with respect to information. At any rate, to whatever extent one assumes that this market functions as indicated, the desirable allocational effect indicated would occur only if there is a free market for stock information.

I have proposed elsewhere empirical tests that would at least give highly suggestive answers to the question of how information values are allocated in the market.[102] For instance, if we found that a group with access performed significantly better in the stock market than some control group, that would suggest that information is a component of the compensation for certain positions. That would not mean that those individuals were realizing a greater-than-market rate of return for their services but only that one component of their income may reflect monopolistic access to information.

III

Disclosure and the Economics of Regulation

After forty years of federal regulation of securities, it is unfortunate that there is no public or political demand that the SEC prove that this legislation has done more good than harm. We no longer live in an era, like the 1930s, when the public accepted government regulation of business as the obvious cure for all economic ills. Today much of the informed public even suspects that industry regulation may be baleful. And even so publicly isolated and obscure an agency as the SEC can be tainted by political scandal.

And yet it is very difficult to imagine who would provide the constituency for this demand on the SEC. Certainly, the established investment banking and brokerage firms have little interest in changing the status quo. But even the interest of securities firms in preserving the status quo is small compared to that of the individuals who would have little to do apart from administering these laws. First and foremost is the bureaucracy itself. As many observers have begun to note painfully in recent years, a governmental bureaucracy is often the strongest single force lobbying for the maintenance and expansion of regulation. After all, as William Niskanen has shown,[103] members of the bureaucracy are in the business of producing and marketing regulation, subject to specialized market incentives and constraints. The social value of their product may be less desirable than that of ordinary markets, but that has little bearing on the motivations and behavior of the participants.

No less directly concerned to preserve the field of securities regulation is the securities bar. This group, through organizations like the American Bar Association and the American Law Institute, has assumed, without opposition, considerable responsibility for law reform in the securities area. At this moment a major project is underway to rethink all the SEC statutes and integrate them into a federal securities code. [104] This effort has probably employed as many public spirited, highly regarded, and well-intended lawyers as ever worked on a similar program of federal law reform. Unfortunately, however, this same group is beset by a subtle conflict of interest that, perhaps unconsciously, influences its every decision. The one thought members of this reform group dare not consider is that the basic philosophy of this entire field of regulation is wrong and that the public would be better off without governmentally controlled information markets.

It is odd that lawyers should so easily ignore for themselves a rule of fiduciary obligation they regularly proclaim professionally for others. This is the doctrine that a person in a position of trust or special obligation must avoid not only profiting at his beneficiary's expense but even giving the appearance of a conflict of interest. The reason for that rule is simply that it is part of the human condition to rationalize and justify solutions that are in our own best interest.

There is no known limit to our ability to justify what benefits ourselves, even though there is no consciousness of harm to others and there is even a strong sense of self-righteousness and personal sacrifice. Few proponents of government regulation of an industry's ethics consciously and cynically ignore the public's interest. Yet industry regulation appears more often to restrain competition and injure the public than benefit them.

So it is with securities law. Lawyers proclaim the desirability of these rules because they sincerely believe that they are benefiting the public. What could be more desirable, for instance, than a "simplification" of securities laws in the form of a federal securities code. Yet, if the results of that codification are anything like our tax laws, the results will be anything but a simplification. The work product will simply create more work for the securities bar and more firmly establish the permanence of that group.

I have tried to demonstrate that there are a significant number of questions to which economists could address themselves on merely one aspect of securities law. Yet, members of the securities bar do not call upon professors of economics and finance to examine these issues or aid them in the process of law reform. Is it because the securities bar is unaware of these issues or because they doubt the ability of other specialists to help? I doubt it. Rather, I suspect, any lawyer making such a suggestion would seem to have "lost his faith." Just as priests are usually the strongest believers in a religious faith, so it is with specialized lawyers. Fellow members of the bar would be less cordial to such a heretic and less willing to consider him, in that term of great professional approval, a "leading securities lawyer."

In a real sense they would be correct. To be a leader of the securities bar, one must be on extremely friendly terms with important SEC staff members and even commissioners. Such a "social" position is not reached automatically by studying lawbooks. Rather, typically, it requires an apprenticeship at the Commission and then practice in one of the important corporate law firms. Then begins the gradual ascendancy through the committee structure of the American Bar Association or related organizations to the exalted position of "leading securities lawyer."

If at any point along the way an individual begins to wonder out loud whether the whole system of regulation is actually in the public's interest, he will not appear to other leaders to have the stuff from which leadership is made. He may also find that he is less able to serve his clients well, since a continuing friendly relationship with the SEC staff is essential to that function. The circle will then be complete, for certainly one cannot be a leading securities lawyer without numerous or important clients.

What, then, of the academics? Do they provide a last hope to be the public's watchdog in the area of securities regulation? For many years the academic side of securities regulation was also dominated by graduates of the Commission. One in particular, Professor Louis Loss of Harvard, is the Chief Reporter on the codification project and has been the towering academic figure in the field for over twenty years. Ambitious young professors, of course, follow basically the same course as emerging leaders at the bar. Until recently few law professors even had sufficient sophistication in economics to raise hard questions in this field. For many of them, therefore, their failure to speak out reflected nothing more sinsister than their not having anything to speak out about.

Still, in the long run, as Joseph Schumpeter once pointed out,[105] it is the business of intellectuals to question the established order. And we are beginning to see some movement in that direction by influential law professors in this field and not merely by troublemakers like myself. These movements are tentative and hesitant to be sure, but they are clearly in the right direction.

But the academic economists, particularly those with a bent for applied work, cannot escape all blame. For the most part, they too have ignored the public's interest in rigorous analytical and empirical work in this field. Of course, there has been no great audience for such work, and it is very costly to gain the legal sophistication necessary to make economic studies in this area meaningful. In almost every empirical study to date on specific aspects of securities regulation there are glaring legal or factual misconceptions that could have been avoided if the authors had been better acquainted with the law in the field, However, I do not wish to carp about these errors, as have several lawyers in the field. The economics scholars should not be thought of as advocates engaged in litigation with the securities bar. Rather the legal scholars should try to find what is correct about these economic studies and useful for legal reform.

We are, to be sure, only at the early beginnings of any broad academic interest in this field, and that interest is fragile. Much of the policy interest that now exists grew from the theoretical works on the random-walk or efficient-market hypotheses, each of which developed for reasons totally unrelated to securities law. Yet that is the nature of many advances in scholarship and of many applications of scholarship to practical affairs.

It is too late for the few skilled economics authorities to have any influence on the current codification project. But if economists turn their attention to this matter now, they may be able to influence the first major reconsideration of that code, which should be due in about 1984.

NOTES

1. L. Loss, *Securities Regulation*, 2d ed. (Boston, 1961), Vol. I, p. 127.

2. W. Cary, *Cases and Materials on Corporations*, 4th ed., unabridged (1969), 341-349.

3. See generally W. Katz, "The Philosophy of Midcentury Corporation Statutes," 23 *Law and Contemp. Prob.* 175 (1958).

4. *Stock Exchange Practices*, Rept. of Com. on Banking and Currency, S. Rep. No. 1455, 73d Cong., 2d Sess. (1934).

5. See H. Manne, *Insider Trading and the Stock Market*, (New York, 1966), pp. 8-10.

6. The following quotes are by SEC Chairman Ray Garrett and appear in 29 *Bus. Lawy.* 9-10 (1974):

We have had cases of fraud and of mismanagement and disregard of investor interest that rival anything known to the men of 1933 who set about to construct a system that would make the world safe for small investors against the depradations of the robber barons, the princes of privilege, the malefactors of great wealth and the just plain bandits of earlier days.

These cases are, in fact, grist for the mill of those chronic non-believers in our whole structure of investor protection through disclosure and maximum reliance on private policing and self-regulation. They enable some to say that our system of securities regulation is an elaborate farce. Except, perhaps, for those features that make it easier for investors to sue, they might urge that we have accomplished nothing significant and that it would save the taxpayers and everyone else a lot of money to junk the whole mess and revert to 1932 and the far more satisfactory philosophy of caveat emptor.

7. SEC v. National Student Marketing Corp., CCH par. 93, 581 (D.D.C., 1972).

8. See *Wall Street Journal*, April 24, 1973, p. 1, col. 6.

9. SEC v. Texas Gulf Sulphur, 401 F. 2d 833 (2d Cir., 1968), *cert. denied*, 394 U.S. 976 (1969).

10. G. Benston, "Required Disclosure and the Stock Market: An Evaluation of the Securities Exchange Act of 1934," 63 *Am. Ec. Rev.* 132, 135 (1973).

11. Discussion by B. Manning, in H. Manne (ed.), *Economic Policy and the Regulation of Corporate Securities* (Washington, D.C., 1969), pp. 81 ff.

12. J. Mofsky, *Blue Sky Restrictions on New Business Promotions* (New York, 1971).

13. See *Wall Street Journal*, February 25, 1974, p. 1, col. 1.

14. See M. Kroll, "Some Reflections on Indemnification Provisions and SEC Liability Insurance in the Light of *Barchris* and *Globus*," 24 *Bus. Lawy.* 681, at 688 (1969).

15. Note to Rule 460, par. (a) under the Securities Act of 1933.

16. Accounting Series Release No. 4. And also note ASR No. 115.

17. Princeton, 1966.

18. Most notably R. DeBedts, *The New Deal's SEC: The Formative Years* (New York, 1964), and J. Landis, "The Legislative History of the Securities Act of 1933," 28 *Geo. Wash. L. Rev.* 29 (1959). And see other authorities cited in the Bibliography of M.

Parrish, *Securities Regulation and the New Deal* (New Haven and London, 1970), which does basically confirm Hawley's conclusion about federal securities regulation.

19. J. Schumpeter, *Capitalism, Socialism and Democracy*, 3d ed. (New York and London, 1950), pp. 84-85.

20. "The American Investment Bankers' Association . . . has endeavored by formulating certain fundamental principles of honest and straightforward statement, to encourage members to offer as complete information to prospective investors as conditions permit." A. Dewing, *Financial Policies of Corporations*, 3d rev. ed. (New York, 1934), p.1018.

Parrish, supra note 18, ch. 1, shows that the Investment Bankers' Association were content with the restrictions on entry to their profession resulting from state laws and saw no need for federal legislation. However, by the early 1930s, the conflicts even within the IBA must have been apparent to anyone in the industry, with the significant split being between the old-line New York houses, plus one or two in Boston and Philadelphia, and the smaller underwriters spread all over the country. The latter's interests probably prevailed then, as to some extent they do now, in the IBA. The larger, older houses, however, may have shown much less antagonism to the 1933 Act as it finally appeared. The most suggestive comments actually appear after the Act was adopted. Parrish, ibid., pp. 229-230, has summarized the matter beautifully, apparently without noticing the economic significance of his own conclusion:

Frankfurter's opinion, expressed in 1933, that investment bankers had nothing to fear from the Securities Act, seemed acceptable to many members of the profession by 1940. The reduction of civil liabilities through formal amendment and the modification of accounting requirements were major factors in winning acceptance for the statute, but so, too, was a growing recognition that the law, effectively enforced, assisted financial operations by policing marginal elements within the industry and by promoting minimum standards of disclosure. During 1934-35, SEC stop orders discouraged private issues, the majority of them fraudulent, aggregating over $20 million. The figure reached $155 million in 1938-39. "Responsible members of the [investment banking] profession," T. H. Sanders concluded, "have less fear that competitors will take business away from them by using less exacting standards . . . calculated to make the preparation of the issue cheaper for the issuer, and . . . presented to the public in a more favorable light than they really deserve. . . . Many members of the . . . profession would be greatly disturbed if adverse court decisions should tend to destroy the salutary influences of the Commission."

A high degree of self-regulation reduced opposition from stock exchanges and over-the-counter dealers to the Securities Exchange Act. In addition, the scope of the SEC's responsibilities under both statutes imposed a coherence upon financial activities that decades of private organization had been unable or unwilling to provide. Before the New Deal many investment bankers outside of New York City had looked upon the New York Stock Exchange as inscrutable and somewhat irrelevant to their own endeavors. Few held such primitive ideas in 1940. The Securities and Exchange Commission drew together and made more intelligible the hitherto chaotic activities of underwriting, distribution, and trading. After 1939, for the first time, representatives of the IBA, the National Securities Dealers Association, and the stock exchanges were conferring through permanent, institutionalized committees sponsored by the commission. The SEC helped to professionalize many corporate functions. "In one month," an accountant noted with astonishment, "the SEC has set ... standards ... for the profession, which years of futile committee work within the professional societies have not been able to produce or even begin to produce."

21. This is not intended to suggest that there are no spillover benefits to various firms in an industry from laws that lessen certain risks for all customers, but we would not normally assume that customers would benefit more from this lower cost of doing business than they would lose by the resulting higher prices charged by the firms in an effectively cartelized industry. Minimum standards, as has been demonstrated so dramatically with the disclosure of financial data, tend rapidly to be maximum standards as well. See Benston, "The Effectiveness and Effects of the SEC's Accounting Disclosure Requirements," in H. Manne (ed.), *Economic Policy and the Regulation of Corporate Securities* (Washington, D.C., 1969), p. 23.

22. W. Hawley, *The New Deal and the Problem of Monopoly* (Princeton, 1966), pp. 205 and 224.

23. "As a general rule, the higher the investment grade of the issue the more colorless and unenthusiastic will the circular appear." A. Dewing, supra note 20.

Also see ibid., p. 1013: "[The circular's] tone must be direct, formal, critical, and it must be absolutely devoid of demonstratives and superlatives. It should merely state facts. . . ." Compare ibid., Bk. III, ch. 8, entitled "The Marketing of Low-Grade Securities". "No specific information is ever given in these [low-grade] circulars, no specific facts, earnings, or capitalization of the new enterprise." Ibid., p. 410.

24. Cf. A. Berle, *Cases and Materials on Corporation Finance* (St. Paul, 1930), pp. 676f.

25. F. Knight, *Risk, Uncertainty & Profit* (New York, 1921), p. 342.

26. See notes 65 infra.

27. G. Benston, supra note 21, p. 28.

28. H. Demsetz, "Perfect Competition, Regulation, and the Stock Market," in H. Manne (ed.), *Economic Policy and the Regulation of Corporate Securities* (Washington, D.C., 1969), pp. 4-5.

29. SEC Exchange Act Release No. 9844 (November 1, 1972).

30. See speeches cited in C. Schneider, Nits, Grits, and Soft, "Information in SEC Filings," 121 *U. Pa. L. Rev.* 254, note 1 (1972).

31. H. Kripke, "The SEC, the Accountants, Some Myths and Some Realities," 45 *N.Y.U. L. Rev.* 1151 (1970).

32. G. Benston, supra note 10.

33. H. Manne, "Accounting and Administrative Law Aspects of Gerstle v. Gamble-Skogmo, Inc.," 15 *N.Y. L. Forum* 304 (1969).

34. See C. Schneider, supra note 30, p. 263.

35. See for a prior mention of this point Comments by R. Rooney in H. Manne (ed.), supra note 11, p. 107.

36. C. Schneider, supra note 30, p. 264.

37. "It may be bruising to the commission's ego, but the undoubted fact is that the most significant information from the standpoint of influence upon the markets is not disclosed in registration statements or proxy statements." A. Sommer, "Comments" in H. Manne (ed.), supra note 11, p. 94.

38. And see ibid., p. 101.

39. See "Disclosure to Investors," *The Wheat Report* (SEC, Washington, D.C., 1969), pp. 95-96.

40. Reference should also be made here to the underlying question of whom the disclosure is really designed for. Is it sophisticated analysts, who then "retail" the information to the investing public, or is it the latter group directly? The answer to this question, which would influence the style and content of every required disclosure, seems fundamental to the whole regulatory area. Yet no single question of policy creates more pronounced symptoms of schizophrenia in the SEC than this one. Ibid., p. 52. Perhaps by never settling the question the agency keeps various enforcement options open. Also by not addressing the issue the Commission certainly avoids a lot of difficult and probably embarrassing admissions that would have to be made. But as desirable government behavior, the approach certainly leaves much to be desired.

41. H. Manne, supra note 33, p. 324; and see SEC Exchange Act Release No. 9844 (November 1, 1972) and C. Schneider, supra note 30, pp. 280ff.

42. A Cohan, *Yields on Corporate Debt Directly Placed* (New York, 1967).

43. Proposed Rule 146, Release No. 33-5336 (November 28, 1972), CCH par. 79, 108 at 82, 402. And see "Comment, Proposed SEC Rule 146: The Quest for Objectivity," 41 *Ford. L. R.* 887 (1973).

44. J. Mofsky, supra note 12; and J. Mofsky, "SEC Financial Requirements for Broker-Dealers: Economic Implications of Proposed Revisions," 47 *Ind. L. J.* 232 (1972).

45. But see J. Hirshleifer, "Where Are We in the Theory of Information," 63 *Am. Ec. Rev.* 31 (1973), for a refinement of this static notion.

46. Cited in L. Loss, supra note 1, p. 122.

47. G. Stigler, "Public Regulation of Securities Markets," 37 *Jnl. of Bus.* 117 (1964).

48. I. Friend and E. Herman, "The SEC Through a Glass Darkly," 27 *Jnl. of Bus.* 382 (1964).

49. E. Shapiro, "Comments" in Manne, (ed.) supra note 11, pp. 253-254.

50. But see G. Stigler, "Imperfections in the Capital Market," 75 *Jnl. Pol. Ec.* 287 (1967).

51. G. Benston, "The Value of the SEC's Accounting Disclosure Requirements," 64 *Acct. Rev.* 515 (1969).

52. See sources cited in C. Schneider, supra note 30.

53. SEC, "In the Matter of Hot Issues Securities Markets," Ad. File No. 4-148 (March 22, 1972).

54. For a history of the development of Rule 10b-5 and its subsequent interpretation as a rule against insider trading, see H. Manne, "Insider Trading and the Administrative Process," 35 *Geo. Wash. L. Rev.* 473 (1967).

55. J. Lorie and V. Niederhoffer, "Predictive and Statistical Properties of Insider Trading," 11 *Jnl. Law and Ec.* 35 (1968).

56. SEC v. Texas Gulf Sulphur 401 F.2d 833, (2d. Cir., 1968).

57. Unfortunately, Lorie and Niederhoffer failed to notice the six-month effect. The failure of many economists doing empirical studies in this area

to integrate institutional and legal nuances plagues almost every economics work in the field. Perhaps one of the reasons so few economists have paid attention to securities regulation is because the lawyers and regulators have so complicated the area that it is not efficiently or cheaply workable by the economists.

58. Most notably, Gerstle v. Gamble-Skogmo, Inc., 298 F. Supp. 66 (E.D.N.Y., 1969). See H. Manne, supra note 33.

59. The only exception to the statement in the text might be found in the current efforts to utilize the proxy machinery to force proponents' notions of corporate social responsibility on unwilling managers. In many of these disputes, the rhetoric of democracy has been heard. See, e.g., D. Schwartz, "The Public-Interest Proxy Contest: Reflections on Campaign GM," 69 *Mich. L. Rev.* 421 (1971); also see Medical Committee for Human Rights v. SEC 432 F.2d 659 (D.C. Cir., 1970). A response appears in H. Manne, "Shareholder Social Proposals Viewed by an Opponent," 24 *Stan. L. Rev.* 481 (1972).

60. G. Benston, supra note 10.

61. A. Sommer, Jr., "Required Disclosure in the Stock Market: The Other Side." Copies of this speech are available from the SEC in Washington, D.C. Also see A. Sommer, supra note 37.

62. All in all, sixteen regressions dealing with various types of financial information were computed for the month when the financial data were sent to the SEC and sixteen for the month when earnings were announced, usually a month before the SEC receives them.

63. H. Kripke, supra note 31.

64. Supra note 61.

65. For the most recent survey of findings in this field, see J. Lorie and R. Brealey (eds.) *Modern Developments in Investment Management* (New York, 1972), especially E. Fama. *Efficient Capital Markets: A Review of Theory and Empirical Work* (New York, 1972), p. 109.

66. The earlier collection was P. Cootner (ed.), *The Random Character of Stock Market Prices* (Cambridge, 1964).

67. W. Baumol, *The Stock Market and Economic Efficiency* (New York, 1965).

68. J. Lorie and V. Niederhoffer, supra note 55.

69. As demonstrated in J. Lorie and V. Niederhoffer, ibid.

70. Of course the strong-form theory necessarily implies that the information was known by someone who either purchased or refrained from selling as a result of the information. Knowing alone is not enough, and since trading (but not holding as a result of a changed reservation price) takes time, the adjustment, as indicated in the text below, cannot always be instantaneous.

71. E. Fama, supra note 65, p. 143.

72. Ibid., p. 150.

73. See especially the comments of R. Schwartz in Lorie and Brealey, supra note 65, pp. 157ff.

74. P. Samuelson, Proof that Properly Anticipated Prices Fluctuate Randomly, 6 *Ind. Mgt. Rev.* 41 (1965).

75. See generally H. Manne, supra note 5, ch. 7.

76. One cannot help reflecting how similar the factors discussed here are to what happens with molecules of gas under pressure. The molecules collide with different intensities and bounce about in the most unpredictable fashion, though none can escape the bounds of the containing vessel. On the average

the strength of all the molecules approaches the limit described by the mean of their forces. I do not mean to suggest that we can carry this analogy very far, but the similarities are quite suggestive, with the pressure effect of the confining vessel being analogized to the last known market price, specialists and insiders.

77. H. Manne, "Our Two Corporation Systems: Law and Economics," 53 *Va. L. Rev.* 259 (1967), and H. Wu, "An Economist Looks at Section 16 of the Securities Exchange Act of 1934," 68 *Col. L. Rev.* 260 (1968).

78. O. Williamson, "Corporate Control and the Theory of the Firm," in H. Manne, (ed.) supra note 11, p. 310, n. 64.

79. See H. Wu, supra note 77.

80. H. Manne, supra note 5, ch. 5.

81. See H. Manne, "Insider Trading and the Law Professors," 23 *Vand. L. Rev.* 547, 587-588 (1970).

82. SEC v. Texas Gulf Sulphur, 401 F.2d 833 (2d Cir., 1968).

83. J. Keynes, *The General Theory of Employment, Interest and Money* (New York, 1936), p. 156.

84. W. Baumol, supra note 67, p. 51.

85. Ibid., pp. 48-50.

86. See A. Alchian and W. Allen, *University Economics,* 2d ed. (Belmont, California, 1967) pp. 89-91.

87. H. Manne, supra note 5, pp. 80ff.

88. See M. Scholes, "The Market for Securities: Substitution versus Price Pressure and the Effects of Information on Share Prices," 45 *Jnl. of Bus.* 179, 182 (1972).

89. Ibid., p. 183, and Alchian and Allen, supra note 86.

90. At least until the purchasing "signals" them that there may be some information warranting a higher reservation price. See M. Scholes, supra note 88.

91. Cf. writers cited in H. Manne, supra note 81, pp. 549ff.

92. E. Fama, L. Fisher, M. Jensen, and R. Roll, "The Adjustment of Stock Prices to New Information," 10 *Int. Ec. Rev.* 1 (1969).

93. Supra note 73.

94. See for a survey of this and similar legal esoterica, R. Reilly, "Inside Information: Much Happening, Little Resolved," *New York Law Journal,* December 10, 1973, p. 38, col. 1.

95. See A. Meltzer, "On Efficiency and Regulation of the Securities Industry," in H. Manne (ed.), supra note 11, p. 217.

96. Consider the following quote from a speech by then SEC Chairman Cohen, cited ibid., p. 229: "Almost every regulatory problem we have concerning the securities markets is related in some way to the level or structure of rates prescribed by the minimum commission rules of the New York Stock Exchange."

97. V. Niederhoffer and M. Osborne, "Market Making and Reversal on the Stock Exchange," 61 *Jnl. Am. Stat. Assn.* 897 (1966). Also see *Wall Street Journal,* "The Market Makers," September 17, 1973, p. 1, col. 6.

98. J. Hirshleifer, supra note 45, pp. 34-35.

99. A. Alchian and H. Demsetz, "Production, Information Costs, and Economic Organization," 62 *A.E.R.* 777 (1972).

100. Cf. J. Hirshleifer, supra note 98, p. 34, answering that there are offsetting monopolny influences on the purchasing side and that the net balance is unclear.

101. A. Alchian and R. Kessel, "Competition, Monopoly and the Pursuit of Pecuniary Gain," in *Aspects of Labor Economics* (Princeton, 1962).

102. H. Manne, supra note 5, at p. 63.

103. W. Niskanen, *Bureaucracy and Representative Government* (Chicago and New York, 1971).

104. L. Loss, "Status of the Federal Securities Code," *New York Law Journal*, December 10, 1973, p. 1, col. 1.

105. J. Schumpeter, supra note 19, pp. 145ff.

WALL STREET IN TRANSITION: THE IMPACT OF THE EMERGING SYSTEM ON SECURITIES TRADING AND THE ECONOMY

Ezra Solomon

Dean Witter Professor of Finance
Stanford University

I do not have a written speech to read to you. This session was labeled a lecture, and I have taken that literally. The written version to be produced later will fill in the "inaudibles," delete the slips of syntax, and add a few footnotes where necessary. It will also contain a separate, shorter paper documenting one of the major points I plan to make today, which does not lend itself to extensive oral presentation.[1]

The lecture format has its advantages and disadvantages. The big advantage is that it is easier to listen to than a recital of a written text. The disadvantage is that one misspeaks, or wanders off at a tangent. But even these lapses might

[1]See "A Note on the Two-Tier Market, 1970-1974" by John G. McDonald and Ezra Solomon, published as part of this volume.

turn out to be a net advantage after all. For
example, misspeaking might lead me to say
something interesting! As Frank Knight used to
say when he held sway at the University of Chicago: Dissertations and other scholarly works
can be divided into two categories—dull and interesting; and the interesting ones can be further
divided into two subcategories—those with com-
putational errors and those with typographical
errors.

The subject assigned to me has an extraordinarily long title. That title encompasses two
quite separate themes, which are sometimes
perceived to be interrelated.

The *first* theme is essentially a *structural*
one and will be treated as such. It concerns the
impact of the transition and change which has
been going on for the past few years on the
marketplace for securities: on who does the
transactions, on how transactions are conducted,
and how and to whom transactions commissions
will be paid.

The *second* theme has to do with the probable impact of those structural changes on the
securities market in an entirely different sense of
the term—on how the level and structure of
security prices is determined and the consequences of that determination for the economy
as a whole.

The first, or structural, theme is a relatively straightforward one. While there has been considerable, and sometimes bitter, controversy within the financial community, including those in government who have oversight in such matters, the basic issues involved are not complex ones. In contrast, the second, or *price* theme is complicated, and for two reasons. It deals with the difficult problem of how common stock prices are and should be formed and with the issue of why those prices are important to society. It also has to deal with the many different ways in which different groups perceive the basic problem of security prices and the influence which structural marketplace changes have on such prices.

THE STRUCTURAL ISSUES

As far as the structural transition is concerned, there is no great dispute about what the issues are, even though there is a continuing dispute on how exactly they should be resolved. The major changes which have been taking place and will continue are:

(1) A growing institutionalization of com-

mon stock ownership and an even more rapid institutionalization of stock trading,

(2) The ending of a long regime of fixed
minimum commissions for stock brokers,

(3) The emergence of a truly central marketplace for stocks with new, but not yet
precisely determined trading rules.

All three developments have been well
documented and therefore do not require much
beyond a descriptive summary statement cover-
ing the nature of the issues, the relationships
among them, and a broad estimate of their probable impact on the structure of the future
marketplace.

Institutional Dominance

The root of recent and ongoing changes in
the marketplace for securities is a rapid rise in
institutional ownership of and trading actively in
common stocks.

The trend toward institutional ownership itself has been going on for a long time. Since
World War II, individual investors, on net balance, have been *net* sellers of common equities,
and institutions like pension funds (managed
primarily by banks), bank trust departments,

and (until recently) mutual investment funds have been *net* buyers. That trend accelerated in the 1960s. As a result, we have witnessed a clear-cut reversal in the relative position of individuals versus institutions as trading participants in the marketplace. A market which ten years ago was about one-third institutional and two-thirds individual, as far as trading volume is concerned, is now about two-thirds institutional and one-third individual.

Within the institutional sector itself, there has developed a growing concentration of common stock holdings under the control of a relatively few large commercial banks.

The emergence of institutions as dominant participants in securities trading has had a profound effect on the old "auction" market for securities as it was described in the typical textbook of the 1950s. That market consisted essentially of individual players, working through brokers who were members of an organized exchange, who matched buy and sell orders on the floor of an exchange, and who charged commissions no lower than those prescribed by the exchange to which they belonged.

Conditions today are quite different. Because institutions typically trade in much larger blocks of securities than individuals, three related changes have taken place. These are: (1) the growing importance of large scale block

trading; (2) the demise of the former system of
fixed minimum commissions set by exchanges;
and (3) an increasing fragmentation of the
marketplace.

Block Trading. In an idealized auction market, when Party A sells to Party B, neither needs
the services of a "specialist" except as a meeting
place where A's broker can contact B's broker in
order to conduct and execute a trade. Occasionally the specialist has to step in as a dealer on his
own account, but only when there is an imbal-
ance between demand and supply of a particular
security on a particular day or week. By doing
so, the specialist provides some evenness to the
marketplace. That, indeed, is his reason for
being.

Two factors encouraged institutional traders to "go around" the specialist and to conduct
trades without his participation. One was the
fixed minimum commission rate that had to be
paid in order to use his services; transactions
outside regular channels provided lower transaction costs. The second factor was that even if
institutional traders were willing to pay the regular commission rate, the exchange specialist had
neither the capital nor the willingness to accept
for his own account their very large net orders
to buy or sell. Those two forces led to the development of active trading of large blocks in second and third markets, i.e., outside regular

exchange channels, including trading with non-members and at negotiated rather than stipulated commissions.

Negotiated Commissions. The emergence of transactions not tied to the rules and practices of the organized exchanges has led to a steady breakdown in the system of fixed minimum commissions. Ever since the original *Button Wood Agreement* of 1792—the only written price-fixing agreement that survived the antitrust laws of this country—member firms of the New York Stock Exchange have been required to charge nonmember market participants at least the fixed minimum commission rate laid down by the Exchange. That rule encouraged large traders to "go around" the Exchange, not only to get the services they needed, but to get it at a lower negotiated commission rate. Member firms, who were bound by Exchange rules regarding minimum commissions, but who found they were losing business because of their inability to compete for institutional transactions, began offering research and other services in exchange for the higher commissions they were required to charge.

Observing these developments, the Securities and Exchange Commission, which has oversight in such matters, became concerned. For one thing, the marketplace was becoming fragmented; instead of all transactions going through one venue, some transactions were occurring on the floor of the Exchange, some off the floor but involving member firms, and some in the third market without benefit of either the participation or the reporting facilities of regular channels. Effective commission charges imposed on transactions became equally fragmented. Some customers, generally individuals, paid the regular fixed commissions laid down by Exchange regulation; others paid the regular commission but received special services in partial compensation for doing so; still others paid only a negotiated commission rate or bought and sold in the third market at a "net" price without any explicit commission charge.

The SEC decided that such a system was neither viable nor fair. It has, therefore, ruled that the older system of fixed minimum commissions should be gradually but steadily unfixed, i.e., steadily moved to a competitive or negotiated basis. The new rule of negotiated commissions for all participants was first applied only to large transactions—those above $500,000. It was next extended to transactions above $300,000. By May 1, 1975, negotiated commissions will be the rule for all transactions—large, small, and middle-sized. In short, the long era of fixed minimum commissions set by exchange authority will soon be dead.

Clearly the new rule of negotiated as opposed to fixed commissions does not mean that every time an individual goes to a broker's office after May 1, 1975, he will have to dicker about what the commission on his particular trade will be. Rather, it will be a competitive market in that every brokerage firm will be free after May 1, 1975, to set his schedule of commission rates as he sees fit. There will undoubtedly be price leaders who will set the "standard" rate that many others will follow, but there will also be mavericks who will break from the standard price from time to time, much as now happens in the rest of the economy.

Market Fragmentation. One undesirable result of the emergence of block trades and the transition away from fixed commissions is that the marketplace for many widely held common stocks has become fragmented. Fortunately, technological developments that have occurred during the past decade make it possible, and indeed feasible, to restructure the fragments into a single unified marketplace again. One predictable result of the changes that we have witnessed is that a truly central marketplace for common stocks will be an operating reality within the next few years.

Toward a Central Market

The new central marketplace toward which we are now moving is essentially a nationwide electronic communications network. The emerging system will provide the two ingredients essential to any efficient securities market: (1) a way to tie together *all* market participants on a truly national basis for the purpose of exchanging information on all bids and offers to buy and sell any security covered by the system, and (2) a way of instantaneously reporting all transactions in any of the covered securities.

In other words, every broker will have access to a communications system that is capable of bringing together and displaying in one location, such as a desk-top television screen, all bids and offers currently available in any market center, including not only the exchanges but nonexchange dealers as well. Likewise, every completed transaction, no matter where it occurs, will be reported through a national network which is accessible to both brokers and their customers.

If fragmentation is to be eliminated, the new system will require new rules in addition to new electronic apparatus. Brokers will have to be freed from constraints with respect to *where* they execute a trade for a customer, including constraints on the size and source of their own commissions. In short, rules will have to be devised which promote the idea that any customer can and will get the best trade available in the country—not just the best trade available on his broker's home exchange nor just the best trade for which his broker can earn a commission.

At present, all of the rules for the new central marketplace have not been worked out. Controversy goes on regarding several issues: (1) Which securities shall be included in the system? (For a start, "all" securities listed on a registered exchange will be included, but that list may later be extended.) (2) Who shall have access to the system? (For a start, all qualified broker-dealers will undoubtedly be included.) (3) Should institutions be allowed membership in the new system? (The probable answer is yes, although equally probably they will *not* be allowed to trade for their own account or the account of their subsidiaries.) (4) Who will control and regulate the conduct of participants? Should it be the SEC itself, a new central body, or should it be left to existing groups such as the several individual exchanges and the National Association of Security Dealers under SEC guidance? Should regulation be uniform or diverse? (5) Finally, who will pay for and control the operation of the new system itself?

Obviously, these last two questions present

the crucial difficulties because ultimately they cover and control all of the still unresolved issues.

In spite of the present confusion on specifics, and the large and conflicting number of legislative bills which reflect that confusion, almost everybody is confident that *some* sort of central market system will be a reality by 1976. There will be a consolidated tape that reports all transactions in a given security wherever it occurs. There will also be a combined quotation system that displays all offers to buy or sell. Whatever the details, it will be a more unified, more truly *national* marketplace than we have had in the recent past.

Two major adjunct developments will contribute significantly to the efficiency of the new marketplace. One would deal with the problem of clearing and settling transactions that have been executed. The other will deal with reporting to final buyers and sellers. Both are worth some attention.

Clearing and Settlement. The present system for transferring ownership from sellers to buyers is essentially a physical one: For many trades, securities are actually delivered by sellers, transported, and then redelivered to buyers. The system has frequently been subject to long delays and errors. The new system will operate either through a central depository or through a

network of regional depositories: Clearing itself
will take place on a continuous *net* settlement
basis, much as now occurs when demand depos-
its are exchanged through the banking systems.
Those who wish to hold physical evidence of
ownership may continue to do so, but *transactions* and their settlement will not be held up by
the need for continental physical transfer.

Individual Accounting. An expeditious and
accurate system for informing customers that a
transaction has been completed on their behalf
is also an essential requisite of an efficient marketplace. Traditionally, each firm, no matter
how small, has tried to run and manage its own
"back office"—as accounting and reporting departments are called. The result has been costly
both to firms and to their customers. In the context of a new central marketplace, back-office
operations will also become more centralized.
Expensive computer-accounting technology not
available on an economic basis for each individual firm could easily become available to groups
of firms, if only they agree to centralize or pool
that aspect of their otherwise competitive business. The trend is clearly in that direction, and,
by the time a central market is in operation,
there will also be a large number of centralized
back-office operations through which most firms
will report to their ultimate customer.

The Problems of Change

The transition to a new set of arrangements in the marketplace has generated a large number of anxieties on Wall Street. Some of the expressed anxieties represent bargaining positions of various groups within the financial community; many reflect genuine uncertainties about the future. All of this is occurring in a context of a serious financial squeeze in the financial industry which has been caused by a sharp fall in security prices and trading activity.

The Brokerage Industry. The number of New York Stock Exchange brokerage firms has fallen from 577 two years ago to 517 today. Some firms have merged, but many have gone out of business. The general expectation is that the number of remaining firms will continue to fall.

Some observers have painted extemely pessimistic scenarios about the future of the brokerage business if fixed commissions are abolished, as now planned, on April 30, 1975. Whether those predictions are bargaining points or genuinely held forecasts is hard to say. One such scenario argues that brokerage, as such, will become quite unprofitable under a system of freely negotiated commissions. As a result, firms will go out of the brokerage business on a very large scale, leaving only a handful of surviving firms: Some will go out of business altogether; others will leave the exchanges and shift to acting as dealers, i.e., buying and selling securities, but on their own account rather than as brokers. The overall message is that the SEC's attempt to aid the individual investor by creating more competition in the industry will end up destroying both competition and the auction market as we know it.

Proponents of negotiated commissions, including the SEC, have not been persuaded by those arguments, and the move to negotiated commissions for public transactions will undoubtedly proceed on schedule. The shakeout of weaker firms will also undoubtedly continue, but to nothing like the extent suggested by the pessimistic scenario outlined above. Most observers believe that what will emerge is a stronger, more competitive and more viable population of broker-dealer houses, including national as well as regional firms, numbering in the hundreds rather than the handful predicted by the extreme scenario.

What Will Happen to Research? Most of the leading brokerage firms now provide their customers with something more than merely effecting transactions: They provide research as well as advice and guidance and considerable bookkeeping, and the customer pays for the entire

"bundle" of services through his commission. Indeed, large institutional investors systematically
allocate the commission dollars they pay for
transactions (known as "soft dollars") on the
basis of the usefulness of the particular attention
and research they receive from brokerage firms.
Some people expect that under a fully negotiated commission system commission rates will
be forced down by practice or law to a bare-
bones minimum level sufficient to cover transactions services only. Research and other associated services, if they are to be performed at all,
will have to be charged for explicitly, i.e., "un-
bundled." The further fear is that customers
may not be willing to pay "hard dollars" for
such services, that droves of research analysts
now employed by brokerage firms will be disem-
ployed, and finally that the small individual investor will find himself completely deprived of
any guidance and information.

All these fears are probably exaggerated.
Some unbundling will occur, but nowhere to the
extent stated above; some research analysis activity will be phased out, but much will remain.
There will be a brokerage-only bare-bones op-
tion for those who want it—just as there are
fourth-class forms of transportation today for
those who want it. But there will be other options as well. Many individuals and most institutional investors will continue to find it worth-

while and possible to pay for extra service, including good research, through commission dollars.

Individual Costs. One assumption that is commonly made is that future negotiated commission rates for small individual investor transactions will be *lower* than fixed rates have been. That is unlikely. The cost of effecting a single transaction is not very sensitive to its dollar size. Under a competitive regime, small transactions may actually cost more than they did a few years ago.

The Role of Commercial Banks. One question which is not related to the particular structural issues being discussed, but which is relevant to the broader question of the future marketplace, is whether commercial banks might or will be allowed to step in to fill any void that would be left at the retail level if traditional brokerage firms collectively fail to adapt smoothly to change. Banks have the resources, the skills, and the degree of public confidence to do what brokers now do, and some have already moved into the securities business in indirect ways. For example, some banks have introduced special investment funds for individuals which allow customers to invest small sums automatically and regularly in certain specified securities. By pooling many orders into a single sizable transaction, banks are able to provide small investors with extremely low transaction costs. The role of banks in the marketplace is one more un-answered question about the future.

IMPACT ON SECURITY PRICES AND THE ECONOMY

I turn now to the other side of the basic question: How have all of the structural changes that are going on affected the market, not as a place where transactions are carried out, but in the broader sense of a place where prices are set and where capital is generated for new young companies or established companies that wish to expand?

The Functions of the Market

There is general agreement that the securi-ties market performs essential and important functions. The functions are interrelated and therefore difficult to separate neatly. They are:

1. The market provides liquidity. An effi-cient secondary market for equities means that permanent or long-term investment in real cor-

porate assets does not have to be financed by
equally permanent or long-term commitments
of funds by any *one* investor. With an efficient secondary market, the funding can be
permanent for investors *as a group*, but it can
be liquid or temporary for any one individual
or institutional investor.

Liquidity itself has many dimensions—for
example, the ease and speed at which equity
claims can be transferred. But one major di-
mension of liquidity is the *price* at which
investors can liquidate their holdings.

2. The basic liquidity function therefore
melds into the second economic function
served by an efficient securities market—the
continuous setting of a price for common
equity shares. There are many reasons why
price and *price behavior* are important.
Among them are the following:

> (a) Price behavior affects the willing-
> ness of investors to buy or hold
> equity securities. Hence it affects
> the ability of corporations to ob-
> tain permanent financing for their
> long-run assets.

> (b) Price affects the "cost of equity
> capital" to companies, and thus it

indirectly determines the minimum rate of return which that company should set in assaying decisions to invest in new real assets. In short, the level and structure of security prices determines the volume and allocation of social resources available for new capital formation.

(c) Third, security prices and behavior affect the real income of many executives.

(d) The securities market also provides the major channel through which new investment funds from savers and investors flows into new real capital formations by corporations over and above that which can be financed internally.

The central questions that need to be answered are:

(1) How well has the existing market fulfilled those four basic functions?

(2) How will the structural changes

that are and will be taking place alter the degree to which those basic functions are fulfilled?

Current Perceptions

The answers to the questions posed above are intrinsically difficult. An additional difficulty is that the answers themselves are confounded by widely held perceptions regarding the behavior of security prices. In short, there are problems as well as non-problems. By nonproblems I am referring to developments which may be problems in their own right but which are not really related to the structural changes we have been witnessing, although they are frequently attributed to them. The five problems most frequently cited are:

(1) The low level of stock prices as a whole and the extremely low level of returns to equity holders over the past five years.

(2) The structure of share prices among public companies—in particular the so-called two-tier market in which a handful of institutional favorites or so-called glamour stocks enjoy extremely high price-earnings ratios while the rest of the stocks enjoy extremely high price-earnings ratios while the rest of the stocks in the market command extremely low prices relative to earnings.

(3) The attendant difficulties of raising new equity capital, especially for the companies whose stocks are out of favor and for new young companies. For example, the number of *initial*

new issues in 1973 was down to just 99 relative to 568 in 1972.

(4) The liquidity problem: Many market participants allege that common stock liquidity is far less today than three years ago.

(5) Finally, the frustration of many fund managers in not meeting portfolio performance objectives during a period in which there has been an increasing emphasis on the continuous monitoring of very short-term results.

All of the problems cited above are genuine enough and painful enough. That is not the issue. Rather, the issue is: Which of them can be traced in any significant way to the *structural* changes that have been occurring in the marketplace? Unfortunately, there has been a widespread tendency to place the blame for all of them on structural causes—on the growth of institutional investment and the power of institutions, on the block trading to which institutional investment gives rise, and even on the reforms in the marketplace such as negotiated commissions.

A careful examination of the facts shows that the attribution of many of the problems to structural changes is quite unfounded. In particular, the first three problems listed are clearly *nonproblems* in the sense that they have very little to do with the structural origins to which they have been repeatedly traced.

The Level of Stock Prices. The period since
late 1968 has been the worst five-year period
since 1937, and 1973, when the *total* return on
holding the Standard & Poor 500 was a *negative*
15 percent, was the worst single year since 1937.
For most market participants, the market returns achieved lately represent the worst they
have experienced in their adult lifetimes.

But the fact is that stock prices in the aggregate have been through equally painful periods
in the past—and long before institutional
investment was around to blame.

During the World War I period, the main
economic variables such as the Gross National
Product (GNP), corporate output and earnings
rose sharply in terms of nominal dollars due
both to real expansion and high rates of inflation. By 1920, for example, dollar GNP was
over 2½ times as high as it had been in 1910; but
the total market value of equities in the early
1920s was actually *lower* than it had been a
decade earlier. It was not till the late 1920s that
equity values rose to a level that was once again
commensurate with the size of the economy.

The same phenomenon occurred during and
after the World War II period. By 1949, dollar
GNP was again over 2½ times the level which
prevailed ten years earlier, and again a large part
of that huge growth was due to inflation. Yet
the market value of equities was not signifi-

cantly higher in the late 1940s than it had been in the late 1930s. It once again took the better part of a decade for equity values to rise to a level commensurate with the size of the economy.

We are now experiencing a third major episode in which equity values lag behind huge increases in the dollar magnitude of economic activity. Today, the level of dollar GNP is about *twice* the level it was in 1965, and again inflation has been a big factor in the rise. Yet the level of equity values is not significantly above the 1965 level. Nobody can know with certainty whether history will repeat itself this time or if or when the market value of equities will again rise to a level commensurate with the dollar magnitude of the economy. But given the evidence I have cited, it is foolish to blame the present painful gap between the level of stock prices and the level of the economy on purely *structural* changes in the marketplace.

The Two-Tier Market. Frustration with the *general* low level of stock prices and the poor performance of most stocks has focused a great deal of attention on the *structure* of stock prices and on the fact that a few stocks have performed better than most. The market, it has been alleged, has two quite distinct "tiers." On the one hand, there is a small group of "glamour" or "large-capitalization" securities

which are relatively heavily held by the large
institutional investors. Those favored stocks, it is
alleged, are doing well, and principally because
the large institutional investors, who have a
heavy stake in them, keep their prices up
through continued purchases. In contrast, the
vast majority of stocks of other sound companies, variously known as "basic" or even "basic
America," have fared poorly; they sell at extremely low price-earnings ratios, and those
ratios keep declining. Somehow the implication
is drawn that the poor performance of "basic
America" stocks is due to the lack of institutional interest. For example, some observers
regard the fact that the common stock of
McDonald's Hamburgers had a higher *total*
market value than U.S. Steel in 1973 as a bizarre
phenomenon which is bound to undermine the
foundations of our entire society! The fact itself
is traced entirely to the perverse and self-serving
behavior of large institutional investors, and
indeed serious proposals have been made to
remedy the state of affairs by curtailing and con-
trolling the investment activities of the major
institutional investors.

The reasoning connecting the *structure* of
equity prices to *structural* factors in the marketplace is as groundless as that which traces the
recent overall level of stock prices to the same
structural factors. There have always been two-

tier markets; indeed, looking back, any market can be divided into two, three, or as many tiers as one chooses. A reasonable analysis of the recent layering of prices needs to go deeper than most of the popular discussions have gone. Empirical analysis is not a topic suitable for oral presentation, but one view of the so-called two-tier phenomen, written by my colleague, John McDonald, and myself, is included as an attachment to my basic paper.

Shortage of New Equity Capital. A third problem allegedly caused by structural changes is that new equity capital raised through the equity market is no longer available for smaller firms. The problem, if it exists, is real enough. Small firms, on the threshold of going public, suffer when the market for new issues dries up. So does the community of broker-dealers who rely on underwriting and distribution commissions from new issues for part of their revenues. But here again there is little reason to *blame* the problem on the disinterest of large institutional investors.

The problem of the shortage of new equity capital is really a problem of price. When the stocks of large, well-known companies such as Ford Motor Company or Texaco are selling at four or six times annual earnings, investors are obviously unwilling to pay more for equity in a small and unknown new company. Nor are the owners of small companies prepared to sell their equity interest to outsiders at such bargain-basement prices. What we have when equity prices are *generally* depressed is not an absolute shortage of equity capital, but a shortage of equity capital at a price that most people regard as fair and reasonable. Exactly the same phenomenon prevailed around 1950 when the "shortage of equity capital" was also a much discussed issue.

Nonetheless, suggestions continue to be made that the present shortage can be corrected by legislating that large funds must invest at least some part of their assets in specified categories of stocks. Such a move is misdirected and is likely to do more harm than good. The alternative and more likely solution is to permit a more widespread flow of information for small issues of small companies through a national quotation network. Such a move will increase the willingness of regional broker-dealer firms to take the initial interest in such issues—and that is where the initial interest rightly belongs.

The Liquidity Problem. While the basic problems of the price level and price structure in the equities market today are not properly explained in terms of structural marketplace changes, there are two other problems which are at least partly related to structural changes.

The first of those problems is the complaint that liquidity has gone out of the marketplace. This is partly a structural issue. A falling market in which a significant number of participants must trade in sizable blocks of stock is one in which the lack of liquidity can be more of a problem than it would be in a market consisting entirely of small investors. The natural unwillingness of block positioners to take long positions in a falling market, and their added unwillingness to do so in the new world of bare-bones commission rates, has contributed to the apparent decline in liquidity. I am not suggesting that block positioning is impossible under a system of negotiated commissions. But in a falling market the positioner requires a relatively high commission as part of his shield against trading losses. However, institutional investors are required to report to their clients and trustees on total commission payments made, and in a world of negotiable (and hence lower) commission rates, such high commission payments are harder to justify.

Likewise, the declining profit margins of broker-dealers and their lack of adequate capital is also a *structural* cause for the liquidity phenomenon. However, the impact of structural factors on the decline in liquidity should not be exaggerated. It is probably partly responsible for somewhat sharper changes that have occurred in the market price of particular securities, but it would be wrong to blame every dramatic price change on the liquidity factor alone. Many such changes are the simple result of the rapid dissemination of new information. Two recent examples come to mind:

On December 21, 1973, Westinghouse stock fell sharply. According to *Business Week,* this was "a concerted institutional bail out: the dumping of Westinghouse Electric Corporation in which the market value of one of America's most famous companies was cut 25 per cent in a single day."

A converse experience occurred on March 14, 1974: Motorola stock rose 25 percent in a single day on the announcement of plans to sell the Motorola television business to Matsushita.*

In these cases it was not a question of lack of liquidity as such, but rather a question of new information. The sharp price changes are both desirable and indeed fair. In contrast, a *gradual* adjustment to the new levels dictated by such new information is *not* a desirable market. It must mean that some poor investor was incorrectly buying or selling at the intermediate

---

*A third dramatic example of rapid price change occurred after this paper was delivered. On May 29, 1974, Polaroid, one of the so-called first-tier "glamour" stocks of 1973, fell 22 percent in one day.

prices! If institutional investors are in fact responsible for sharp, rather than gradual, changes to a new stock price level that is much higher or lower than that which prevailed *before* relevant new information became available, they ought to be praised for contributing to a more efficient market rather than blamed for wrecking it!

The Performance Measurement Syndrome. A second problem which is related to *structure* is the modern passion for measuring investment performance. The United States has always had a passion for recording and measuring anything even remotely measurable, and measurement as such is therefore unassailable, at least in principle. But it can do short-run harm, and in my opinion it has, as far as portfolio performance is concerned.

During the 1960s, we discovered that the computer, properly programmed, could measure the annualized rate-of-return performance on any portfolio, both rapidly and cheaply, for as short a time interval as anyone might possibly desire. The competition among brokerage firms (and their advisers) to provide useful statistical services to the funds whose commissions they sought, plus the competition among potential money managers for clients, has led ineluctably to the almost continuous measurement, ranking, and publication of several "performance" measures over very short-run intervals of time. That, in turn, has led to an incessant pressure for almost instant performance.

Common stock investment, at best, is a long-run game, and always has been one. The recent craze for frequent, explicit and published rankings of "who did best last month or last quarter" seems to have made it extremely difficult for most investment funds to think in long-run terms. I have recently taunted many investment fund managers with the following, purely hypothetical, question (as only an academic can afford to do): "If you were forced to make *one* set of buy or sell decisions today and no subsequent decision to buy or sell until March 1977, what would you do?" Almost everybody's reply is, "That's easy—I would buy U.S. equities." In fact, given the real world choice of timing purchases or sales, and given the watchful eye of the monthly performance measuring computer, most managers appear to be moving into cash.

Of all the *structural* problems affecting the level and structure of stock prices, the measurement syndrome problem is probably the single most important one. It is also one for which even the academic has no answer at all—except that, in the long run, basic long-run values must prevail.

A NOTE ON THE TWO-TIER MARKET, 1970-1974

John J. McDonald* and Ezra Solomon*

*Graduate School of Business, Stanford University.

The image of two or more "tiers" in the market valuation of common stocks has gained wide acceptance in the financial press in recent years. This note illustrates with empirical evidence some of the apparent sources of dismay on the part of portfolio managers and other observers of the capital market in the United States, without attempting definitively to resolve all of the issues relevant to earnings expectations, risk, and return. The two-tier characterization of the structure of share prices was fostered in the period 1971-74, when a relatively small number of stocks appeared to sell for significantly higher price-earnings (P/E) multiples than the majority of issues listed on the New York Stock Exchange. Although the market prices and P/E multiples of many of these so-called first-tier stocks have declined over the past year, the linguistics of "tiers" in the market has not been abandoned. For example: "It is becoming increasingly clear that as long as institutions dominate the marketplace, 'two-tier' markets are here to stay. Only the nature of the stocks in each tier will change."[1] This statement exemplifies the growing awareness that if stocks are perceived to exist in tiers, then the composition of those tiers is indeed likely to change over time.

The present paper reports some evidence on a sample of thirty common stocks listed on the New York Stock Exchange—fifteen companies widely regarded as first-tier companies in early 1973, and fifteen companies considered members of the second-tier majority. We examine data from 1970, before the two-tier characterization was commonplace; in 1973, at the peak of the phenomenon; and again in early 1974, with the most recent data available. In the context of the sample we consider the following question: After one attempts to account for intercompany differences in risk, what part of the increase in P/E multiples in the first-tier stocks in 1970-73 was associated with increased expectations of future growth, and what part represented a higher valuation (coefficient)

placed on the growth variable by market participants? That is, to what extent did the two-tier
perception of P/E ratios appear to be explained
by measures of expected growth and risk in
1970, 1973, and 1974? In mid-1973, when the
two-tier market phenomenon was widely discussed by institutional investors and legislators,
divergent opinions about the current valuation
and likely future performance of common
stocks reflected basic differences in conception
of the return-generating process in the stock
market—representing views of market reality or
world views which we will briefly differentiate.

The Notion of Tiers

Higher tiers are often associated with those
stocks having higher current P/E multiples. Valuation theory suggests that the ratio of current
price to current earnings will be positively associated with *expected* growth and negatively associated with risk; if two stocks are perceived to
be of equal risk, the one with the higher expected future growth in earnings will sell for the
higher multiple of current earnings, here defined
as earnings per share as reported in the previous
four quarters.

In addition to the association with higher P/E ratios, the first-tier delineation has sometimes been used to describe stocks with high *realized* appreciation in market price in recent months—usually associated with new information and revised expectations of investors. Ex post facto there will always exist a group of stocks with unanticipated revaluations during a year and, after the fact, one may partition stocks or industries into two, three, or N tiers based on recent performance. Recent price appreciation and current price-earnings ratios are not, of course, independent; stocks with unanticipated increases in expectations and market price often sell for above-average current P/E multiples. Consider the following industries, which might have been characterized as members of the first-tier in 1967 and 1968, two years during which Standard & Poor's 500 stock index increased by 9 percent and 8 percent: Hotel chains appreciated in market price by 265 percent in 1967 and 53 percent in 1968; toy manufacturers rose by 181 percent and 110 percent in these two years; real estate stocks increased 111 percent in 1967 and 112 percent in 1968. These examples simply serve to remind that before the tier characterization came into vogue in the 1970-74 period, there were nonetheless stocks and industries in every previous period which might have been viewed ex post facto as members of a first tier, in terms of high price-earnings multiples and recent market returns.

Often the tier language carries with it implicit assumptions about the likelihood that the current state of tier-rankings will continue. Such assumptions have led some market critics to exhortations that "something should be done about it" in 1973 and 1974.

Divergent World Views in Mid-1973

Interpretations of market reality in the summer of 1973 obviously reflected heterogeneous expectations on the part of investors and other observers about the future of stocks, particularly those most prominently discussed in connection with the first and second tiers of New York Stock Exchange stocks. It seems useful to identify three divergent "views of the world" which were demonstrated in mid-1973.

World View I reflected a basic assumption that the levels and structure of share prices at the end of July 1973 were, in a deep sense, abnormal and unsustainable—but that time and new information could be expected in the normal course of events to change the anomaly. One major trust company prepared the indices of first-tier and second-tier stock prices, shown in Figure 1. The first tier was identified as the *S & P 15* and the second tier as the *S & P 485*, the remaining stocks in Standard & Poor's 500 stock index.

Adherents to World View I held that the recent performance of these first-tier stocks and the apparent "gap" between the mean P/E multiples in the first and second tiers were not "warranted" by their fundamental valuation calculations, based on their own best estimates of future earnings and dividends. Accordingly, investors in this camp in July 1973 felt that the apparent gap between the two groups of stocks in Figure 1 was likely *to narrow* in 1973-74, as general market expectations reflected in stock prices were revised downward for the "institutional favorite" first-tier stocks relative to the majority of securities in the second tier. Mean P/E ratios expected to persist in the future had not significantly changed from their 1970 levels, in this view, so that the unexpected increases in the P/E ratios of first-tier stocks in 1970-73 were likely to be followed by "reversion toward the mean" in the ensuing months of 1973-74.

World View II reflected the belief that price pressure from continued institutional demand for the stocks in the first tier was a sufficient condition for the apparent gap in share prices of the so-called first and second tiers in mid-1973

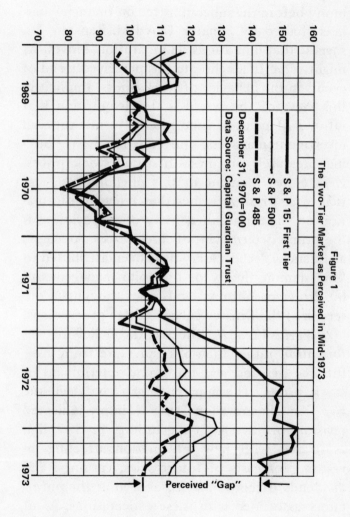

Figure 1
The Two-Tier Market as Perceived in Mid-1973

S & P 15: First Tier
S & P 500
S & P 485

December 31, 1970=100
Data Source: Capital Guardian Trust

Perceived "Gap"

to persist or even *to widen.* Some of the testimony before the subcommittee on financial markets chaired by Senator Lloyd M. Bensten, Jr., suggest that limitations on institutional investors might serve to ameliorate this perceived trend of events in the behavior of stock prices. Implicit in this view of the world is the assumption that inflows of pension fund money to institutional investment managers, and concommitant "buying pressure" on these first-tier stock prices, were a key element in this phenomenon, and that *price pressure* rather than relevant information on the economic activity of corporations is the prime determinant of stock prices. Attempts at financial scapegoatery have been attributed to "the demon theory of portfolio management" by Professor Murray[2] and other thoughtful observers of the Bensten subcommittee proceedings.

World View II reflected the belief that *information* rather than price pressure from institutional demand was the prime determinant of stock prices. The apparent "gap" between the two tiers, illustrated in Table 1, simply indicated revision of investor expectations in 1971-73, associated with new information affecting investors' forecasts of future sales, earnings, and dividends of corporations, as well as the uncertainty associated with these expectations. As of July 1973, this view held that first-tier stocks were neither more nor less "vulnerable" to

Table 1

SAMPLE COMPANIES

*First-Tier Stocks**	*Second-Tier Stocks†*
American Home Products	Alcoa
Avon	AT & T
Burroughs	Campbell Soup
Coca Cola	Caterpillar
Eastman Kodak	Champion Spark Plug
IBM	Continental Can
Kresge	DuPont
Eli Lilly	Exxon
Merck	General Motors
MMM	Johns-Manville
Polaroid	Lone Star Industries
Proctor & Gamble	PPG Industries
Sears Roebuck	RCA
Warner Lambert	Reynolds, R. J.
Xerox	U.S. Steel

*S & P fifteen as shown in Figures 1 and 2.
†Sample from S & P 485 shown in Figures 1 and 2.

decline in price in the next year. Accordingly, the gap which appeared to exist between first-tier and second-tier stocks was expected *neither to increase nor to decrease*, given the similarity of average risk of stocks in the two groups. Expected future returns to investors in common stocks, in this view of financial markets, are primarily a function of risk.[3]

World View III is implicit in the greater part of the recent Department of the Treasury report by Professor Lorie.[4] The efficient-market hypothesis suggests that all relevant public information is reflected in current stock prices. Stock prices at every moment in time are "correct" in the sense that they adjust quickly to new information and reflect the "average" expectations of professional analysts and investors at that time in the market. Institutional investors' desire to buy or sell given stocks is important in this view only if it conveys an "information impact" sufficient to change the expectations of other investors. Information provides the first-order effect on stock prices, and block supply-demand or price pressure per se provides the second-order explanation of stock price changes.[5]

Some bank executives have expressed their conviction of the limited impact of trust department operations in the ultimate determination of share prices, suggesting an inability to "support" the share prices of first-tier stocks.[6] It is noteworthy that the notion of market efficiency implied by World View III, which not long ago represented a decidedly minority view, is generally consistent with the statements of bank officers in defense of their usual role as price-takers in the market. A recent editorial in the *Wall Street Journal* addressed the "powerful forces toward efficiency" in a statement consistent with the set of beliefs implicit in World View III.[7]

Valuation Model

A large part of the two-tier characterization of the market has been phrased in terms of P/E ratios, so that it seems useful to focus on some key determinants of value in this context. A simple valuation model can be used to examine the relationship of expected growth and risk to current price-earnings multiples. Previous work by Malkiel and Cragg[8] indicated that a model of this form can be expected to explain about one-half of the total variance in P/E multiples in a larger cross-section of New York Stock Exchange stocks. Current P/E ratio at a given moment in time is expressed as a function of two variables, expected growth in earnings per share and risk, related to P/E ratios by three coefficients a_0, a_1, and a_2 :

$$P/E = a_0 + a_1 \text{ (Exp. Growth)} + a_2 \text{ (Risk)}$$

The theory of value leads one to expect the estimate of coefficient a_1 to be positive and a_2 to be negative. Estimates of a_1 made at different times in the market may be expected to differ, of course, because of changes in interest rates associated with varying economic conditions and other factors.

Sample

The thirty companies which constitute our first-tier and second-tier samples are shown in Table 1. The first-tier firms are those identified in 1972 by Capital Guardian Trust Company as the S & P 15 of prominent "top tier" companies, as indicated in Figure 1. The sample was quite clearly identified "after the fact," once the two-tier market characterization had become widespread. Each of these firms had large total market value and common stock which had exhibited extraordinary price appreciation since 1971, in addition to the high P/E multiple commonly associated with the first tier. A Morgan Guaranty Trust Company official described many of these first-tier stocks as "recession-proof companies,"[9] with dominant product-market positions in a segment of the economy.

The fifteen second-tier companies were selected as a sample from the remaining 485 companies were designated as the S & P 485 in Figure 1. Some are representative of the "cyclical companies"[10] often associated with the second tier, e.g., Alcoa, General Motors, and Lone Star Industries. It bears emphasizing that studies of the time-series behavior of earnings have indicated that nearly all companies are more or less "cyclical," tending to move in terms of profitability in consonance with economic activity.[11] Among the less cyclical companies in the sample are AT & T, duPont, and Exxon. While the first-tier sample seems reasonably representative of the "consensus first tier" discussed by institutional investors in the 1970-74 period, the reader is cautioned that the second-tier group in Table 1 represents only a small sample of those stocks considered at the time to fall in the second-tier category.

Measurement of the Variables

Expected Growth. Expectations of future growth in earnings and dividends held by "the" market represent an obvious abstraction in the context of valuation. The literature of finance lends one to be cautious in two respects. There is considerable evidence that past earnings growth rates provide only limited information about future growth rates;[12] and analysts' predictions of earnings growth rates in general appear to offer only limited improvement over extrapolations of past growth rates, in predicting future growth in earnings.[13]

Expected growth rates in the present study were taken from the *Value Line Investment Survey*. The estimate of future earnings per share, three to five years hence, was used to compute a percentage expected growth rate over this entire period. The degree to which the Value Line forecasts are representative of "the" market expectations is an open question; there is some evidence that these forecasts may be "better" in general terms of predictive power that those analysts' predictions studied earlier by Cragg and Malkiel.[13] Observations of growth expectations were made at three periods: September 1970, March 1973, and March 1974.

Risk. The volatility of common stock returns to investors relative to the S & P 500 stock index, Sharpe's beta, was used as a measure of risk. Estimates of beta were based on sixty observations of monthly returns. Many investors still feel more comfortable at a deep intuitive level with more traditional measures of business risk (earnings variability) and financial risk (leverage). Beaver, Kettler, and Scholes have demonstrated that the anticipated positive relationship exists between beta, as a market measure of systematic risk, and the traditional accounting measures of risk including earnings variability and financial leverage. [15]

The mean beta of first-tier and second-tier stocks, as well as the variability of quarterly *returns* (dividend yield and capital gain) to investors, were remarkably similar in these two samples, as indicated in Table 2; mean beta was slightly higher for first-tier stocks (0.99 versus 0.97), while total variability of return was slightly lower for first-tier stocks (0.102 versus 0.125). By contrast, the variability of quarterly percentage changes in *earnings* appeared to be dramatically higher in the case of the second-tier companies. The impression shared by some institutional investors in this period that the first-tier "glamour growth stocks" had lower risk appears to have been associated more with the variability or "riskiness" of the time series of quarterly changes in earnings rather than quarterly returns.

P/E Ratios. The ratio of price to earnings was computed from data published by Standard & Poor. The price of each stock on the last day of the month was used on each of the three observation periods. The sum of the last four quarters earnings per share announced prior to the end-of-month date was used in the denominator of the P/E ratio. The reader should note that Value Line does not publish their figures for expected earnings growth on the same day

Table 2

COMPARISON OF RISK MEASURES

	First Tier	*Second Tier*
Systematic Risk		
Mean Beta, as of March 1974*	.990	.970
Variability of Returns for individual Stocks		
Cross-section Mean of standard deviations of individual stock returns,† 14 quarters ending March 1974	.102	.125
Variability of Returns of Tier as a Portfolio		
Standard deviation of quarterly mean returns for the tier (15 stocks) over 14 quarters	.076	.080

*Based on five years of monthly data, relative to S & P 500 index.
†Return comprised percentage dividend yield plus capital gain or loss in quarter.

Table 2 *(continued)*

COMPARISON OF RISK MEASURES

	First Tier	*Second Tier*
Variability of Earnings Changes for Individual Stocks		
Cross-section mean of standard deviations of percentage quarterly earnings-per-share changes for 15 individual stocks over 14 quarters ending March 1974	.351	1.002
Variability of Earnings Changes of Tier as a Portfolio		
Standard deviation of quarterly mean earnings changes for the tier (15 stocks) over 14 quarters	.193	.654

for all stocks, so that observations of P/E ratio are consonant in time, but those of expected growth are not precisely consonant as postulated in this cross-section model.

Empirical Findings

An overview of the two-tier phenomenon may be obtained from the description of variable means in Table 3. From September 1970 to March 1973 the mean P/E multiple of the first-tier sample increased from 29.0 to 46.1, while the mean P/E ratio of the second-tier sample declined slightly from 12.8 to 12.1 over this period. Expected growth rates, initially higher in the first-tier sample, increased for both groups. From 1970 to 1973, three-to-five-year expected growth rates increased by nine percentage points in the first-tier sample of six percentage points in the second-tier sample.

From 1973 to 1974 expectations of growth in the first tier appeared to remain unchanged, as reflected in the Value Line growth rate forecasts; in this twelve-month period the mean P/E multiple declined to the 1970 level of 29.1 for this first-tier group. For the second-tier sample in the period March 1973 to March 1974, both growth-rate expectations and P/E multiples declined.

In the three years 1970-73 *realized* mean growth rates reported by second-tier companies were 79.2 percent, representing significantly higher growth than the 47.3 mean rate attained by the first-tier group. In contrast to this

Table 3

PRICES EARNINGS RATIOS, EXPECTED AND
REALIZED EARNINGS GROWTH AND
REALIZED RETURNS TO INVESTORS, 1970-1974

	First Tier Mean	Second Tier Mean
Price-Earnings Ratio*		
September 1970	29.0	12.8
March 1973	46.1	12.1
March 1974	29.1	9.7
Expected Earnings Growth		
September 1970	53.3%	48.8%
March 1973	62.5	54.9
March 1974	62.5	29.1
Realized Earnings Growth		
1970-1973	47.3%	79.2%
Realized Return on Common Stock†		
September 30, 1970 to March 31, 1974	49.3%‡	24.4%‡

*Last 4 quarters reported earnings per share.
†Over-all percentage dividend yield plus capital gain in period.
‡Standard deviations of returns in each 15-stock sample were
similar: 37.0% and 34.8% in the first and second tiers.

apparently superior record of average earnings growth produced in 1970-74 by the second-tier companies, returns to investors in the first-tier group exceeded that of the second tier; overall returns on common stock, ignoring reinvestment of dividends, were 49.3 percent for the first-tier and 24.4 percent for the second-tier stocks. Investors in second-tier stocks faced the following apparent paradox: Earnings growth rates of the second-tier companies were both higher than expected and higher than realized by the first-tier firms, yet realized mean rates of return to investors in the common stocks were only half that of the first-tier stocks in this period of three and one-half years.

Regression Results

The valuation model relating current P/E ratios to expected growth and risk generally "fit" the data on the first-tier stocks far better than the data on the second-tier sample, as indicated in Table 4. The percentage of variance in P/E ratios explained in the model was 48 to 88 for the first tier and zero to 16 for the second tier. The estimated regression coefficients were generally insignificant in the case of the second-

Table 4

REGRESSION RESULTS FROM
VALUATION MODEL, 1970–1974

Dependent Variable: P/E

| Date | Sample | Estimated Coefficients | | | R^2 |
		Con-stant	Expected Growth	Risk	
Sept. 1970	First Tier	9.27 (1.88)*	.100 (1.93)	14.59 (3.46)	.51
	Second Tier	15.99 (5.75)	.005 (−.13)	−3.04 (− .93)	.00
Mar. 1973	First Tier	18.84 (3.25)	.324 (7.94)	7.07 (1.07)	.88
	Second Tier	16.31 (3.81)	.033 (.95)	−6.18 (−1.64)	.11
Mar. 1974	First Tier	21.51 (3.84)	.162 (3.78)	−2.53 (− .45)	.48
	Second Tier	12.48 (3.69)	.067 (1.92)	−4.85 (1.39)	.16

*Numbers in parentheses are t-ratios.

tier cross-section; the model with these measures of the variables simply provides little empirical insight into the valuation process, beyond the weak finding that the estimated coefficients of growth and risk and the anticipated sign in five of six instances.

More important, the estimated growth term coefficient for the first tier increased from 0.100 to 0.324 between 1970 and 1973 at the peak of the discussion of the two-tier market. In the ensuing year 1973-74, this coefficient decreased to 0.162, in the direction of its 1970 magnitude. In sum, the increase in first-tier P/E multiples from 1970 to 1973 was due in small part to an increase in expectations of growth and in large part to a higher valuation (coefficient) placed on those expectations.

Findings for the risk variable appear to conflict with results anticipated from the theory of value. Beta was positively, rather than negatively, associated with P/E ratios in 1970 and 1973 after expected growth was accounted for. In 1974, the sign of the risk variable was negative, as we would normally expect. In sum, this structural model and these data suggest that the upward valuation of the first-tier stocks from 1970 to 1973 is not adequately explained by increased in expectations of growth, after intercompany differences in risk have been recognized.

Expected, Unexpected, and
Realized Earnings Growth

Realized earnings growth in 1970-73 may be considered ex post facto to comprise two components: expected growth and unexpected growth. Note that the Value Line expectations in 1970 related to three-to-five-year growth, so that the time horizon is not precisely specified; realized growth rates in 1970-73 may be comparable to the lower end of the three-to-five-year spectrum covered by these expected growth rates. The data in Table 3 support the inference that realized earnings growth exceeded expected growth in the three years 1970-73, and that the *unexpected* component of growth was larger for second-tier companies than for the first-tier firms. As of September 1970 mean *expected* growth rates for the two tiers were 53.3 percent and 48.8 percent for the three-to-five-year time horizon; after the fact, mean *realized* growth rates in the three years 1970-73 were 47.3 percent and 79.2 percent in the first- and second-tier samples.

In appraising these events, it is useful to consider alternative models of the process by which earnings changes are generated. One conceptual view of the process, explored by Beaver, suggests that corporate earnings behavior over time may be well approximated by a pure mean reversion process.[16] If this were so, unexpected earnings changes would have no effect on investors' assessment of the mean growth rate in the earnings generating process of a firm. Unexpected increases in earnings, as we observed with the second-tier stocks in this period, would not affect investors' expectations of the mean of the earnings growth rate distribution for a given company. Unexpected increases in the P/E ratio—or decreases in the E/P ratio of earnings deflated by stock price—would be likely to be followed by reversion toward the man value of the ratio. Alternatively, Ball and Watts[17] have argued that growth rates of earnings per share (undeflated by price) are well approximated by a "random walk." It bears noting that the Beaver hypothesis of long-term mean reversion of E/P ratios is not inconsistent with Ball and Watts' contention, as the latter was concerned with each firm's earnings relative to its past history, while Beaver's tests were concerned with cross-sections of E/P tiers. Empirical findings based on monthly data for 1949-68 in Beaver's seminal study suggested that mean reversion in E/P ratios took place over an 8-year period.

Earnings and Price Change Results, 1973-74

As of mid-1973 the first-tier stocks had been widely identified and discussed; price appreciation from October 1970 to June 1973 and high P/E ratios as of mid-1973 had been used in large part to *define* this first tier. While the expectations of institutional investors were obviously diverse, the high P/E ratios of first-tier stocks reflected expectations by "the market" that future earnings growth would be higher for these stocks than for the second-tier sample. Furthermore, the essentially equal mean beta estimates of systematic risk for the two samples imply *ex ante* market expectations of stock price appreciation which were equivalent for these first and second-tier samples. If these market expectations had been realized subsequent to June 1973, stock prices would have increased by the same percentage in the two groups, while earnings would have grown at a higher rate as expected in the first-tier sample, leading quite naturally to a "narrowing of the gap" in P/E ratios. It is important to stress that even without a closing of the apparent "gap" in *price* indices in Figure 1 as of mid-1973, there might have been a narrowing of the difference between mean P/E ratios in the ensuing quarters as the greater *expected* growth in first-tier earnings was actually experienced.

We turn now to the actual earnings and price change results in 1973-74, shown in Table 5. In the three quarters subsequent to June 1973, the mean P/E ratio of the first-tier stocks declined substantially for two reasons: the mean earnings change of the first-tier stocks was 21.3 percent, and the mean price change (net of dividends) was −21.1 percent between June 1973 and March 1974—hence the numerator declined and the denominator increased in the P/E ratio. The second-tier stocks experienced a mean change in earnings per share of −14.5 percent and a mean price change (net of dividends) of 6.2 percent in the three quarters ending March 1973. In the same period, the return on Standard & Poor's 500 index was −7.36 percent.

Among the 15 first-tier stocks in these three quarters, 40 of the 45 earnings figures were higher than reported earnings in the comparable quarter of the previous year. Unanticipated price declines in the first tier appeared to be due to some downward revision in expectations of future earnings, while the actual mean earnings change was positive over the period June 1973 to March 1973. Many companies in the first-tier sample, including IBM, Avon, Polaroid and others, announced "new news" of an unfavorable character in the latter period. In the case of the 15 second-tier stocks, returns were positive while mean earnings declined. A large component of the earnings declines appear to have been viewed by "the market" as *transitory* in the second tier sample.

In sum, the realized returns on the first-tier stocks were lower than those on the second-tier sample, as also reflected in a narrowing of the apparent "return gap" in the price indices shown in Figure 2 in June 1973 to March 1974. While these adverse price changes in the first tier may have been anticipated by some adherents to World View I, as of mid-1973, they were obviously not expected by "the market" as a whole. By contrast, the superior realized growth in earnings of first-tier companies was in part expected by "the market", as indicated by higher P/E ratios at a given level of risk in mid-1973; as this first-tier growth was in fact realized, the "P/E ratio gap" between the two tiers tended to decline, as expected in an efficient market context.

Conclusion

This note on the structure of the two-tier phenomenon, as seen from various viewpoints, is intended to be exploratory in nature. As the two-tiers were in large part defined by price

Table 5

EARNINGS CHANGES AND COMMON STOCK RETURNS SUBSEQUENT TO
WIDESPREAD DISCUSSION OF "TWO-TIER" MARKET IN MID-1973

	Third Quarter 1973	Fourth Quarter 1973	First Quarter 1974	Total Three Quarters*
First-Tier Stocks (15)				
Mean Change in Earnings per Share from pervious quarter (%)	8.4	18.9	-13.2	21.3
Number of EPS increases†	8/13	8/14	6/13	7
Number unchanged EPS	2/0	1/0	1/0	0
Number of EPS decreases‡	5/2	6/1	8/2	8
Mean Return on Common Stock (%)	-3.5	-14.2	-4.7	-21.1
Number of Positive Returns	5	0	2	1
Number of Negative Returns	10	15	13	14

Second-Tier Stocks (15)

Mean Change in Earnings per Share from previous quarter (%)	-6.3	17.3	-22.2	-14.5
Number of EPS increases†	5/13	9/13	3/9	5
Number unchanged EPS	2/0	0/0	0/0	0
Number of EPS decreases‡	8/2	6/2	12/6	10
Mean Return on Common Stock (%)	15.2	-12.8	5.7	6.2
Number of Positive Returns	14	2	11	11
Number of Negative Returns	1	13	4	4

*Product of three quarterly changes.

†Number of increases relative to previous quarter/number of increases relative to same quarter in the previous year.

‡Number of decreases relative to previous year/number of decreases relative to same quarter in the previous year.

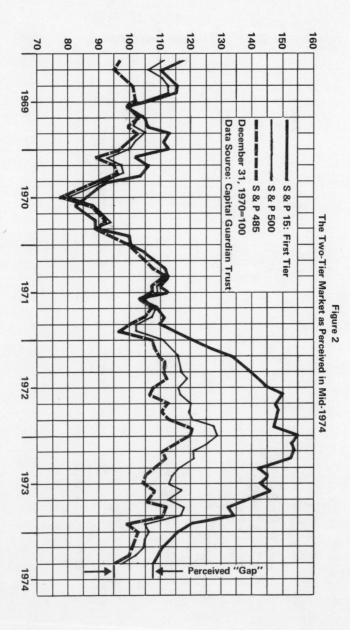

Figure 2
The Two-Tier Market as Perceived in Mid-1974

S & P 15: First Tier
S & P 500
S & P 485
December 31, 1970=100
Data Source: Capital Guardian Trust

Perceived "Gap"

appreciation and P/E ratios up to mid-1973, it is useful to focus on subsequent earnings and price changes. In doing so, one must distinguish between the "narrowing of the gap" in prices or returns, shown in Figures 1 and 2, and in P/E ratios. Given the similar mean (beta) risk levels of the two samples, the price changes expected by believers in World View III were the same for both tiers, but the expected earnings increase was larger for the first tier; hence, some "narrowing of the gap" in P/E ratios was anticipated, while a "narrowing of the gap" in price indices was not anticipated in World View III for the period June 1973 to March 1974.

Whatever the sequence of events that led to the structure of share prices in mid-1973, there were a number of heads of institutional investment firms who, as adherents to World View I, argued publicly at the time that a "mean reversion" tendency was to be expected in 1973-74, with an attendent narrowing of the "gap" both in prices and P/E ratios. In the context of World View III, these spokesmen in 1973 were to be regarded as "belief deviants" who proved to be correct in 1973-74 either by skill or by chance—some of whom may even have had a sort of functional fixation on historical earnings-price relationships. For believers in World View I, however, forecasters of a narrowing of the two-tier price "gap" were not extraordinarily lucky, but had simply viewed the current situation in 1973 at the height of the two-tier phenomenon with the detached perspective that allows a masterful observer to discern peaks of sentiment on the part of the crowd whose majority expectations are reflected in stock prices. Examination of quarterly data does not permit us to conclude definitively that the evidence supports either World View I or III, to the exclusion of the other. However, most observers would agree that World View II rested more on frustration and was advocated more with cant then detached consideration of the evidence. The subtle problem in interpreting the two-tier phenomenon as of mid-1973 was that while stock prices reflected investors' current expectations in the basic sense of market efficiency, the apparent increase in the "gap" between the two groups of stocks from 1970 to 1973, in terms of P/E ratios and returns, was not well explained by actual earnings changes, earnings growth expectations reflected in the Value Line data, or perceptions of risk. The data on earnings and price changes from June 1973 to March 1974 are consistent either with World View I or, in the context of generally unanticipated "new news," with World View III.

All of science, including the behavioral science of economics and finance, accords a high value to successful puzzle-solving. The two-tier market phenomenon has been illuminated along a number of dimensions in this note, but not "solved." It remains to be demonstrated why the upward revision in P/E ratios and prices of the stocks, later to be called first-tier, took place in 1970-73—why the valuation coefficient of expected earnings of these first-tier stocks increased as much as it appeared to from 1970 to 1973 and declined again in 1973-74. Progress in our understanding of the world very often comes from awareness of *anomaly*, i.e., that nature and mankind have somehow violated our expectations as governed by our world view. [18]

The process we have addressed in the 1970-74 period was by no means anomalous in the singular sense—"tiers" of one description or another have existed in every market period. An interesting problem is to explain the emergence of a new first-tier of securities in terms of unexpected increases in P/E ratios and stock prices in those cases where the "fundamental" variables of expected earnings and risk do not appear to account for these increases. Anomalies in valuation—called *bubbles* in their more extreme forms in earlier times—are identified only after the fact as we perceive reality in World View III. A major puzzle still to be formulated centers around the explanation of financial bubble phenomena in this sense, as they may occur in markets which we see as efficient in terms of aggregate experience. A great deal is known about the time-series behavior of stock price changes and earnings in statistical terms, and this body of literature strongly supports the paradigm of market efficiency embodied in World View III; the earnings portion of the closing of the P/E gap is consistent with the latter view. Just as Aristotle warned that one sparrow does not make a spring, one narrowing of a perceived price "gap" between two samples of stocks obviously cannot validate or invalidate a view of the world. Adherence to a world view is based on *belief* and commitment which are not easily altered by new fragments of evidence. Believers in World View I have generally been reinforced by the sequence of events characterized as the two-tier market in 1973-74; many adherents to World View II have been quieted; and many of us who are believers in World View III will remain persuaded that the data—particularly in larger samples—are consistent with an efficient market interpretation of the phenomenon.

NOTES

1. "The New Two-Tier Market," *Business Week* (April 6, 1974), 52.

2. Roger M. Murray, "Institutionalization of the Stock Market," *Financial Analysts Journal* XXX (March-April 1974) 19.

3. The seminal theoretical papers on the risk-expected return relationship are those of William F. Sharpe, "Capital Asset Prices: A Theory of Market Equilibrium under Conditions of Risk," *Journal of Finance* XIX (September 1964), 425-442, and John Lintner, "The Valuation of Risk Assets and the Selection of Risky Investments in Stock Portfolios and Capital Budgets," *Review of Economics and Statistics* XLVII (February 1965), 13037. Empirical evidence that institutional portfolio returns do in fact vary with risk level was presented by Michael C. Jensen, "Risk, the Pricing of Capital Assets, and the Evaluation of Investment Portfolios," *Journal of Business* XLII (April 1969), 167-247 and John G. McDonald, "Objectives and Performance of Mutual Funds, 1960-1969," *Journal of Financial and Quantitative Analysis* IX (June 1974).

4. James H. Lorie, "Public Policy for American Capital Markets," *Department of the Treasury* (February 7, 1974).

5. See Myron S. Scholes, "The Market for Securities' Substitution versus Price Pressure and the Effects of Information on Share Prices," *Journal of Business* XVL (April 1972), 179-211. The secondary effects of intraday price pressure in block trading were reported by Alan Kraus and Hans Stoll, "Price Impacts of Block Trading on the New York Stock Exchange," *Journal of Finance* XXVII (June 1972), 569-588.

6. See Samuel R. Callaway, "The Two-Tier Market Reexamined," *Wall Street Journal* (September 28, 1973) for an analysis of the two-tier market by the head of Morgan Guaranty Trust Company's Trust and Investment Division.

7. "Market Efficiency," *Wall Street Journal* (April 17, 1974) 18.

8. Burton G. Malkiel and John G. Cragg, "Expectations and the Structure of Share Prices," *American Economic Review* LX (September 1970), 601. A review of other cross-section studies of this gender may be found in Frederick W. Bell, "The Relationship of the Structure of Common Stock Prices to Historical, Expectational and Industrial Variables," *Journal of Finance* XXIX (March 1974), 187-197. It should be emphasized that choice of accounting methods may also account for differences in P/E ratios; for example, see William H. Beaver and Roland E. Dukes, "Interperiod Tax Allocations and Delta-Depreciation Methods: Some Empirical Results," *The Accounting Review* XLVIII (July 1973) 549-559.

9. A recession-proof company was perceived to be "a company able to maintain growth in earnings and dividends even during economic down-turns," owing to "a product or service with a growth trend strong enough to carry through a business slump, a big enough order backlog to last through the down part of the business cycle, or perhaps a flow of income sustained by customers' payments of equipment rentals." Samuel R. Callaway, op. cit. The empirical validity of this recession-proof company characterization has yet to be demonstrated.

10. Samuel R. Callaway, op. cit.

11. Philip Brown and Ray Ball, "Some Preliminary Findings on the Association between the Earnings of a Firm, Its Industry, and the Economy," *Empirical*

Research in Accounting: Selected Studies, 1967. Supplement to Volume 5, Journal of Accounting Research, 55-77.

12. See, for example, John Lintner and Robert Glauber, "Higgledy Piggledy Growth in America," in James Lorie and Richard Brealey (eds.) *Modern Developments in Investment Management* (New York; 1972), 38.

13. John G. Cragg and Burton G. Malkiel, "The Consensus and Accuracy of Some Predictions of the Growth of Corporate Earnings," *Journal of Finance* XXIII (March 1968), 67-84.

14. Fischer Black, "Yes, Virginia, There is Hope: Tests of the Value Line Ranking System," *Financial Analysts Journal* XXIX (September-October 1973), 11-14; John G. Cragg and Burton G. Malkiel, op. cit.

15. William H. Beaver, Paul Kettler and Myron S. Scholes, "The Association between Market Determined and Accounting Determined Risk Measures," *The Accounting Review* XLV (October 1970), 654-682.

16. William H. Beaver, "The Time Series Behavior of Earnings," *Journal of Accounting Research,* Supplement (Autumn 1970), 62-99. This paper dealt primarily with various measures of earnings deflated by price.

17. Ray Ball and Ross Watts, "Some Time Series Properties of Accounting Income," *Journal of Finance* XXVII (June 1972), 663-681.

18. Thomas S. Kuhn, *The Structure of Scientific Revolutions* (Chicago, 1970), 52.

DISCUSSANT

Kalman J. Cohen

Since the speech by Professor Ezra Solomon is fresher in our memories, I shall start with some comments concerning his talk. Then I shall briefly turn to the speech by Professor Henry G. Manne.

Professor Solomon noted that there are three major structural changes now taking place in the securities industry:

(1) the growing institutionalization of the market for common stocks;

(2) the ending of fixed minimum brokerage commission rates;

(3) the emergence of a central market for common stocks.

These changes are indeed important, and I would not dispute Professor Solomon's

187

judgment that they are the most important structural changes now occurring in the American stock market. I must point out, however, that there are some additional major structural changes already taking place which are also going to exert profound impact on Wall Street and the securities industry in the United States. These additional structural changes include:

(4) the increasing internationalization of securities trading and financial flows;

(5) the increasing overlap in the functions performed by various financial institutions and some other types of business firms;

(6) the reduced ability of the New York Stock Exchange to cartelize the market for common stock.

A major structural change now occurring in the American securities industry is the growth in foreign competition stemming from the increasing internationalization of securities trading. Foreign competition for American securities firms is increasing in two different ways. First, many Americans are now investing some of their funds in foreign securities markets. Some American securities firms will obtain part of the business that results when American invest their money abroad, but many foreign securities firms will also get some of that business. Second, we are now seeing, and will continue to see, an increase in the number of foreign securities firms

doing business in the United States. In part these
foreign securities firms serve as a conduit for
portfolio investment from abroad flowing into
the American market, and in part they help
facilitate foreign direct investment in American
business and industry. In addition, these foreign
securities firms will also increasingly compete
for what has been traditionally thought of as
domestic American brokerage and underwriting
business.

There is much evidence that overseas
markets are becoming increasingly inter-
nationalized. The underwriting of new securities
issues across national boundaries is growing. The
activities of American investment banking firms,
as well as American commercial banking firms,
have increased overseas, in connection with the
offshore financing requirements of multinational
corporations. An important question to raise for
the American securities industry is, How well
will it be able to accommodate to these changes
in the international investment pattern? What
should Wall Street be doing to anticipate and
react to these changes? What sort of competition
does the American securities industry expect
from foreign securities firms, both in the
American as well as in overseas markets?

The next major structural change that Professor Solomon did not note, but which I feel has profound implications for the future of Wall Street, is the increasing overlap of functions performed by various financial institutions and also by some business firms not traditionally regarded as financial institutions. Professor Solomon did briefly raise a question as to whether commercial banks will begin to perform a more active broker-dealer function at the retail level. The answer, I feel, is clearly yes. Indeed, through Edge Act subsidiaries and affiliates, American commercial banks are already active in underwriting and trading corporate securities overseas. Domestically, developments like monthly stock purchase plans and dividend reinvestment plans represent back-door ways in which American commercial banks have begun to perform a retail brokerage function. In the future, I believe that there will be increasing ways in which American commercial banks are going to compete more actively with traditional securities firms. This will be a healthy development.

It is also interesting to note that some business firms, not normally thought of as financial institutions, are increasingly performing financial functions. For example, such giant retailing firms as Sears Roebuck, Penney, etc., are now extending more consumer credit than are the commercial banks. Moreover, a firm like American Express is not thought of as a financial institution domestically, but of course it is a major bank overseas. Further, the increasing development of diversified financial service companies, whether they have commercial banks or insurance companies as their base, is going to have profound impacts on the competition faced by the more traditional Wall Street broker-dealer firms.

The final additional aspect of structural change which Professor Solomon did not mention but which I feel will have profound impact on Wall Street is the reduced ability of the New York Stock Exchange to cartelize the market for common stocks. This aspect of change is perhaps not as evident as the others discussed today, but nonetheless, it will become increasingly prevalent and apparent in the future. Many developments that the Securities and Exchange Commission has been pushing in recent years, such as the elimination of fixed minimum brokerage commission rates and the movement toward a central market where all potential market makers and traders will have fair treatment and equal access, are reducing the importance of the "club" formed by New York Stock Exchange members. Unfortunately the New York Stock Exchange itself is overly resistent to change. Rather than recognizing the inevitability of the forces now at work and trying to create opportunities to continue the leadership of the New York Stock Exchange (although in a transformed mode), the Exchange is exhibiting a dinosaurlike resistance to change. This will precipitate the demise of the Exchange as a major force in the future American securities industry.

Let me now turn to some of the points with which Professor Solomon and I are in agreement, in order to examine some of their further implications. The individual investor is now playing a smaller role in the stock market than formerly, and indeed, he probably will continue to play an even smaller role in the future. Many people on Wall Street think that this is bad, because it reduces their commission revenues. From an economy-wide rather than a vested-interest perspective, however, this means that there is substantial excess capacity in the securities industry. This is especially true with respect to those firms maintaining expensive retail distribution networks oriented toward serving small investors. Inevitably, this will lead to increased exiting of firms from the securities industry, as Professor Solomon has predicted. I believe that a substantial proportion of this exiting will come from the more retail-oriented broker-dealer firms.

Professor Solomon and I agree that a reduction in the number of securities firms is not necessarily bad. It is an inevitable consequence of the reduced activity by individuals in the stock market. There are many economic reasons, involving tax incentives, the dissemination and analysis of information, portfolio diversification, etc., why the small investor is often much better off to do his investing in common stocks through financial intermediaries rather than investing directly in the stock market.

Professor Solomon and others have pointed out that institutional dominance makes the stock market less liquid than it formerly had been when individuals played a larger role. Anecdotal evidence is often cited concerning sudden, large changes in prices that have occurred when institutions seem to act in concert to buy or sell a particular stock. Less often cited are the systematic studies that have been conducted on the impact of institutional investors on market price volatility. In those cases where there has been no real news concerning the changing prospects of a company, stock price changes due to institutional buying or selling of 50,000 or 100,000 shares are relatively small, in the order of a few dollars per share, and relatively temporary. But in those cases where there has been a great deal of institutional trading reflecting relevant news, e.g., decreased earnings prospects of a company, then the stock price drops quickly by a large amount, and it tends to stay at the new lower level rather than going back up soon afterward. This type of sharp market price drop in reaction to bad news is really desirable, and it is characteristic of the way in which an efficient market should perform. In the past, when institutions were a less important factor in the market, there were many individual investors who would act as "fall guys" for the institutions. In other words, as the institutions (with their better analysts, closer access to information, etc.) reevaluated the prospects of a company and began to dump its stock, there were individual investors in the market who were willing to pay considerably more for the stock than its inherent worth.

Clearly, price stability and market liquidity are not the same. Large, rapid price changes should sometimes occur, and these typically reflect relevant news rather than lack of liquidity. Thus, the type of institutionalization that is now taking place in the American stock market probably represents a desirable development as far as true market liquidity and the efficient impounding of news into market prices are concerned.

I believe that considerably more analysis is needed in order to determine how well the stock market performs its main economic function, which is the allocation of capital resources. This is another question briefly raised by Professor Solomon. It is clear that in the past decade there have been relatively few new equity issues. What are the reasons for this? Does the increasing institutionalization of the stock market account for this? Professor Solomon thinks it does not, and I agree with him.

There are many reasons, perhaps the most important being the tax incentives of corporate debt, that can explain the relative lack of new equity issues without any need to invoke the increasing institutionalization of the stock market. Professor Solomon has also blamed the relatively depressed price of corporate equities for this phenomenon. In addition, some of the retail-oriented broker-dealer firms will point out that new equity issues, especially those of small and growing companies, are really merchandised and sold rather than being bought. If this viewpoint is correct, one might wonder whether new and smaller companies are going to continue to have access to the equity market, given our prediction of increasing institutionalization of the stock market and a reduction in the number of retail-oriented securities firms.

I do not think that this will be a problem in the future. I have great faith in the ingenuity of the American free enterprise system. If on average, investments in new and growing companies

are attractive on a risk-adjusted basis, then I
think that there will be devices developed to
encourage such investment despite increasing
institutionalization. Some of these devices may
be increasing use of venture capital funds, the
provision of appropriate tax incentives, imagina-
tive institutional packaging techniques, etc., and
these will result in new equity issues being
absorbed to the extent that they offer
appropriate profit opportunities to investors.

Professor Solomon has discussed the central
market, and I would agree with most of what he
has said about it. There is one important aspect
concerning the central market that has not yet
been discussed today, and that is whether a
specialist in a stock will have a monopoly position (as the New York Stock Exchange would
like to maintain), or whether competing specialists or market makers in a stock will be per-
mitted (as the National Association of Security
Dealers and various third-market makers advo-
cate). I personally believe there are sound economic reasons for permitting specialists to
compete in a given stock in the central market.

In commenting on the differences between
auction markets and dealer markets, Professor
Solomon implied that dealer markets were less
efficient and less desirable. However, this is not
necessarily the case. There are highly efficient
dealer markets, e.g., the market for United

States government securities and the over-the-counter market for some major national corporations that qualify for listing on the New York Stock Exchange but do not choose to be listed. Such dealer markets appear to be highly efficient in all relevant respects.

It seems clear that the central market could be a combined auction/dealer market. This has been suggested by Professor Morris Mendelson in his monograph, *From Automated Quotes to Automated Trading: Restructuring the Stock Market in the U.S.* (New York University Institute of Finance, *The Bulletin*, Nos. 80-82, March, 1972). The system that Professor Mendelson sketches would in effect be an auction market for relatively small trades in lots of a few hundred shares, and a dealer market for larger trades. These two types of market can be effectively combined into a single computer-based market system. There would substantial advantages in the liquidity and "best-price" characteristics afforded to individual investors dealing in the auction market from the simultaneous existence of a dealer market in the same computer-based trading system.

Let me now briefly discuss a few of the points raised by Professor Manne. With regard to the Securities and Exchange Commission and required disclosure, I believe the situation that we now have is fundamentally different from the situation that existed in the 1920s and the early 1930s. In particular, I feel that the vast information and analysis industry that is now associated with the stock market has come to rely upon SEC filings as a means of verifying information. Furthermore, SEC requirements provide incentives for firms to disclose information. This is part of the mechanism that helps to make the market efficient. I cannot believe that there would continue to be the same types of market efficiencies that we now take for granted if the SEC were suddenly to be abolished. With respect to the implications of the research of Professor George Benston (that Professor Manne has cited) on this matter, I believe that at most a Scotch verdict is appropriate: The impact of the SEC and its disclosure requirements on the stock market has been "not proven" rather than having been "disproven."

It may well be, as Professor Manne has stated, that during the Great Depression the SEC tended to reduce competition in the securities industry. But it is clear that the SEC has had the opposite impact in recent years. It is the SEC that has been the prime driving force toward negotiated and reduced brokerage commission rates, toward the introduction of a composite tape, and toward the ultimate development of a central market. Without pressures from the SEC, the ability of the New York Stock Exchange to cartelize the securities industry would remain greater than it now is. If we really did abolish the SEC and its disclosure requirements, as Professor Manne advocates, I am afraid we would be throwing out the baby with the bath water.

An important future challenge to the SEC, which has not yet been mentioned today, concerns the extent to which they should regulate and what disclosures they should require from foreign firms whose securities are traded in the United States capital markets. It remains to be seen whether the future posture of the SEC toward foreign firms will stimulate or inhibit the use by foreign firms of the American capital markets.

To summarize my position with respect to the SEC, I do not believe that the correct solution is what Professor Manne advocates, i.e., its immediate abolition. Rather, we should admit that the SEC has not been perfect, and that its present disclosure requirements may not be optimal. The real challenge is then how to modify and improve the disclosure requirements and regulatory functions of the SEC to increase the efficiency of securities markets and to bring the SEC's behavior more in line with modern economic and financial theory. But simply to eliminate the SEC would, in my opinion, be a serious step backward.

DISCUSSANT

William J. Baumol

First, I should start off by pointing out that Professors Solomon's talk has put me in a most embarrassing position, since, as a critic, I find myself agreeing with about everything he said. However, Professor Manne's paper has given me something to chew upon, and I will do my best to take advantage of it. Now in saying that, I want to be careful in delimiting the area of disagreement between myself and Professor Manne, because it is much more important that one remember the valuable things he said, even if one disagrees with him to the extent that I will. The points he has made are far from obvious; I think most of them are fundamentally valid, and certainly they are highly important.

He argues that the regulations on disclosure were ill-conceived, badly designed, and that they may have done, and in fact probably have done, more harm than good. He suggests they have in fact kept out of the market a number of small and highly risk-prone entrepreneurs, and, in the present state of the United States and the world market, that may be a luxury we can ill-afford. He implies that the SEC was instituted with the tacit consent of those regulated firms that were better established because they welcomed the opportunity to discourage the entry of trouble-some competitors. Certainly, the record of regulation in other fields offers prima facie evidence suggesting that regulation tends to talk of its adherence to true competition while working as effectively as it can to keep it under restraint. Evidence offered by Professor Manne implies that whatever information has been provided under the disclosure requirements has produced very few benefits.

And yet, despite the persuasiveness of these three arguments—that is, the view that regulation generally has not encouraged real competition, that disclosure seems to have produced very little benefit, and the allegation that the requirements of disclosure seem to have arisen out of motivations less than pristine pure—I nevertheless arrive at a conclusion rather different from Professor Manne's. I do agree with him that more information is *not* always better; certainly an infinite amount of information is never worthwhile. After all, additional information always yields diminishing returns and involves increasing costs, and these two must always be balanced off to produce what I have once described as a regime of optimally imperfect decision-making.

Nevertheless, the optimal amount of information while not infinite, is not zero either. Moreover, caveat emptor is not really to me an acceptable rule for public welfare. Reality does display cases of fraud, deception, and dangerous self-deception. There *is* misleading advertising and misleading packaging. I do want groceries to date perishable products and to report unit prices. I do want restaurants to be required to display the results of the most recent sanitary inspection. And incidentally, we should take note of the number of restauranteurs who consider that requirement to infringe their fundamental liberties.

Caveat emptor can indeed be very dangerous to the public. A notable case in point was brought out by a student who recently conducted an investigation of surgery that was carried out under two different plans—one in which the surgeons were paid a fixed fee per month, and the other in which the surgeons were paid by the operation. The difference in frequency of operations per thousand between the two areas was literally on the order of magnitude of four to one.

Surely, the public ought to get some information about that sort of situation. How, indeed, can the consumer protect himself without some sort of disclosure requirement. My conclusion, therefore, is that there may well be need for major reform in the disclosure process. I think that Professor Manne has given us very good reason to look for that sort of reform. But reform is not tantamount to abolition. Surely, at the very least, prohibition of deceptive advertising is appropriate, and perhaps a little more than that is required.

It seems to me that the issue to which Professor Manne should lead us to address ourselves, therefore, is not *whether* information should or should not be provided, but *how much* and what sort is really most appropriate to serve the public interest.